MONEY TALKS

PRACTICAL WISDOM FOR
BECOMING FINANCIALLY FREE

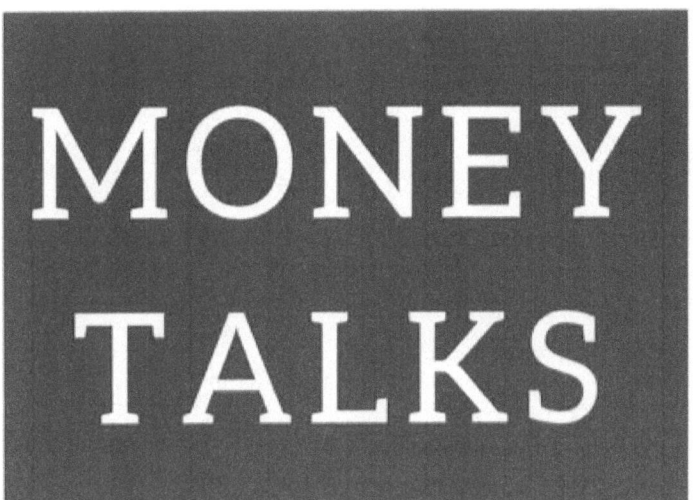

MARK CONNER

Copyright © 2018 Mark Conner

2nd Edition 2025

All rights reserved. This book or any portion thereof may not be reproduced or used in any manner whatsoever without the express written permission of the publisher except for the use of brief quotations in a book review.

Published by Conner Ministries Ltd

Additional copies of this book may be purchased from:
www.amazon.com/author/markconner

Email: mark.conner7@icloud.com
WEB: www.markconner.com.au

Unless otherwise indicated, all quotations from the Bible are from the *Holy Bible: New International Version*®. NIV®. Copyright ©1973, 1978, 1984 by International Bible Society. Used by permission of Zondervan. All rights reserved.

Scriptures marked NLT are taken from the *Holy Bible, New Living Translation*. Copyright ©1996, 2004, 2007 by Tyndale House Foundation. Used by permission of Tyndale House Publishers, Inc., Carol Stream, Illinois 60188. All rights reserved. Used by permission.

Scriptures marked TLB are taken from the *The Living Bible*. Copyright ©1971. Used by permission of Tyndale House Publishers, Carol Stream, Illinois 60188. All rights reserved.

Front cover designed at www.canva.com

ENDORSEMENTS

"Countless books on how to use money compete for readers. It is easy to find complicated ones. It is common to find those that just promote getting rich, even by so-called Christians. There are plenty of theoretical studies that are hard to apply and how-to-manuals not based in good theory. But where does one find a short, practical, biblically grounded, clearly written little book that addresses all the important questions about using money in Christian ways with up-to-date charts, graphs and statistics to back everything up? Mark Conner has now written it. Get a copy. Devour it. Then live it out."

Craig L. Blomberg
Distinguished Professor of New Testament. Denver Seminary, Littleton, CO

"It is often not productive to ask pastors for their views on finance or financiers for their views on pastoral care. It is therefore very refreshing to read Mark Conner's 'Money Talks: Practical Principles for Becoming Financially Free', which blends the insights of the pastor with the practical applications of someone who has thought carefully about the power that money has over us. He tackles the biblical road map to freedom in financial matters with a persuasive skill and hands on application."

Ken Costa
Author: God at Work

"Mark Conner has written a fantastic book about money and generosity. Many today are looking for wisdom to help us navigate the tensions we face in income inequality, stewardship and wealth, and to reflect the heart and wisdom of Jesus when it comes to our resources. Theologically strong, yet immensely practical, Mark does this so well. I highly recommend this book to you."

Jon Tyson
Church Planter and Author. Church of the City New York.

"Mark Conner has a wealth of experience when it comes to the vital subject of how Christians should handle their money. In this practical guide to saving, spending and giving, he helps us view our finances from God's perspective. He eloquently explains where our hearts should be focussed and offers biblical financial principles that stand the test of time. It's a timely antidote to this age of conspicuous consumption."

Tim Costello
Former Chief Advocate, World Vision Australia

"Money Talks is a concise guide to financial freedom based on brilliant biblical teaching. Mark Conner shares practical Scriptural insight from years of teaching that can help you get free for the traps that keep us from living the generous life we want to live. If you want to be financially free God's way, read Money Talks!"

Dave Ferguson
Lead Pastor - Community Christian Church, Chicago USA.

"Mark Conner is a gifted speaker, writer, church builder and a helper of people to be transformed. His biblical and practical insights concerning money are fresh, proven and easy to apply. Read it, pray it, live it."

Dr. Frank Damazio
International Speaker, Best-Selling Author, Leadership Trainer

"Mark Conner's capacity as a leader is only outweighed by his honesty, big-heartedness and integrity. In the chapters of this book we see his authenticity jump off each page. "Money Talks" is not only accessible and well researched - it is REAL! His down to earth teaching is heaven sent - a balm for the fiscally frazzled!"

Rob Buckingham
Senior Minister, Bayside Church Melbourne

"In the time I have known Mark, his strength of character, leadership and deep understanding of biblical teachings have had a profound impact on my life. Mark's ability to translate complex issues into simple and actionable disciplines is a rare gift, and it is one that he delivers in a deeply personal and authentic way. One of the many principles that Mark has taught and practiced both in his personal life and church leadership role, is financial freedom. As a student of Mark's teaching, I have witnessed individuals and families transform their financial situations from being hamstrung with credit card debt to owning their own properties and running successful businesses. With the wisdom contained in these chapters, I am confident that reading this book will challenge your perspective on biblical stewardship and provide you with the tools to achieve true financial freedom."

Dan Daniels
Founder and Global CEO Daniels Health

"This is a timely and significant book about managing our money well. Mark provides practical ideas to help us improve our thinking about money as well as our daily practices. This book is a great read!"

Lisa McInness Smith
Global Keynote Speaker. Best-Selling Author. Transformational Coach

"Finances can be the F word for many of us, but Dr Mark Conner is a person to trust when it comes to making sense of financial headaches. From million dollar budgets in some of largest churches to standing with people living in extreme poverty, Mark has seen it all. With 7 in 10 people currently living on less than $10 a day and disparity between rich and poor creating global instability, this book could not be more urgent or important. This book will especially help us Christians in rich countries to take stock, pray, think and find imaginative ways to be a solution to injustice in the world by making the most of God's resources at our disposal. Please read this practical, prophetic book and act on Mark's advice. It will help us all."

Rev Dr Ash Barker
Director, Newbigin School for Urban Leadership (NewbiginHouse.uk)

"God's design for people is that they flourish in life, yet because of flawed responses to money, and inadequate understanding about proper financial management, many fall short of His desire for them. That's why I'm glad Mark Conner has created an excellent resource to help people handle finances, with a holistic, biblical approach. I have witnessed firsthand the growth, blessing, and progress of a local church, and its people, who thrived under Mark's leadership; where these life-giving principles were applied. Read this book. Apply these truths. Watch the effect on your personal world and beyond."

Wayne Alcorn
Senior Pastor, Hope Centre; Former National President, Australian Christian Churches

"This book by Mark Conner is well written and thus easy to read; it gives a comprehensive account of what the Bible says on poverty and wealth, and it is full of wise and practical advice for Christians on giving, saving and spending. Everyone who reads this book will find much to think about and every group that studies it will find much to discuss."

Dr. Kevin Giles
Anglican Pastor, Theologian and Author

"My good friend Mark Conner has proven to be a brilliant leader and effective communicator. His well-researched material on finances in this new book will be an enormous help to people everywhere, including families, church leaders and business owners. I highly recommend it."

Phil Pringle
Founder of C3 Church Global; Founding Senior Pastor of C3 Church Sydney

"It has been my experience that the most successful people I know are the most generous people also, why because primarily they have mastered the art of Fiscal Responsibility and acknowledge the true source of their wealth comes from God Himself, therefore they are both proving and living out the Biblical Principle of 'Faithful in Little, Trusted with Much' when it comes to the issue dealing with money in their lives. I commend Mark on how he has dealt with the issue of money in such a sensitive and practical way. It is full of God's truth and wisdom and provides great insight on how anyone can become a generous giver and a faithful steward of His Resources in your life."

Mike Jeffs
CEO and Founder of The Australian Christian Channel

"I welcome this book with all of my heart! As a pastor of a large congregation that contains people who are both rich and poor, lazy and diligent, I know the need of biblical teaching that gives a wholesome and balanced view on money. The wisdom and practical advice Mark Conner offers will be a great help for anyone who looks for better order and more of God's blessings in their finances."

Mats Ola Ishoel
Senior Pastor, Word of Life Church, Moscow

"Mark Conner is a very gifted and globally renowned communicator and in 'Money Talks' he has created a much needed and refreshingly easy to read book with lots of clear illustrative stories and quotes that can help you to bring about transformation in your finances. With Mark's practical and easy to follow teaching, this is an ideal book for you to use as a blueprint on how to become financially free. The combination of financial and spiritual education has never been more critical than in today's high debt culture. This book is full of wisdom and insight. Highly recommended!"

John Sikkema
Executive Chairman, Halftime Australia, Melbourne

"Mark Conner is a great friend in life and ministry, and throughout the years I have grown a great trust and respect in his gift and ability to make divine wisdom accessible, and able to affect our daily lives. As a pastor, I constantly see the need of solid, Bible-based teaching in the tricky area of finances, where many times Christians have ended up either in the ditch of financial fear and an ideal of poverty or in an unsound emphasis on material prosperity. In this book, Mark excels in pointing the right way, and bringing a sound and solid message that truly has the capacity to bless, inspire and actually change your path for the better. I recommend it wholeheartedly!"

Joakim Lundqvist
Senior Pastor, Word of Life, Sweden

"Mark is a great teacher. You will find this to be true if you have listened to any of his sermons or read his books. And he has done it again! Unpacking the truth about money in such amazing ways. You will enjoy this book wherever you are in your financial condition. Thank you, Mark, for taking the time to share your knowledge and to help us all do better in our finances."

Jeffrey Rachmat
Founding Senior Pastor, Jakarta Praise Community Church, Indonesia

"I have enormous respect for Mark Conner. Not only does he bring a wealth of knowledge as a seasoned leader, he also brings an uncanny insight into scripture and humanity that allows him to communicate in such a way that you think to yourself, "Why didn't I see it like that before." Mark has a gift as a communicator which stems from his relationship with God and his understanding of people. He can turn this capacity in many directions to help people. In this book he turns it in the direction ion of people and money. As always he is practical, insightful and imminently accessible. Many will be blessed and better positioned as a result of this work. Mark, the body of Christ thanks you."

Dale Stphenson
Senior Pastor, Crossway Baptist Church

ABOUT THIS BOOK

Those of us who live in the Western world live in some of the richest countries on the planet yet, despite this fact, many people are under financial pressure. In this book, Mark Conner shares practical principles for becoming financially free and living wisely with the resources we have. Learn fresh insights about earning, saving, investing, debt reduction and spending wisely. The book also includes extra material on alleviating poverty, church finances, fundraising and the purpose of business.

TABLE OF CONTENTS

Money Talks	11
1. Poverty or Riches?	15
2. A Story About A Shrewd Manager	23
3. Your Personal Money Makeover	29
4. The Power of a Budget	33
5. Income - How to Acquire Money	35
6. A Plan for Financial Freedom	49
7. Giving - The Power of Generosity	51
8. Saving and Investing - Preparing for the Future	67
9. Spending - Living Within Your Means	77
10. Wrapping It Up	89
Prayers for Financial Blessing	97
Appendix 1: Reflection and Discussion Questions	99
Appendix 2: God's Heart for the Poor and Vulnerable	103
Appendix 3: Church Finances	109
Appendix 4: Fundraising Tips	123
Appendix 5: The Purpose of Business	143
Appendix 6: Recommended Resources	157
About Mark Conner	163
Other Resources from Mark Conner	165

MONEY TALKS

I have a confession to make. Most pastors like me get a little nervous when speaking about two particular topics - sex and money. Yes, it's true. I have decided to save the sex talk for another time (or for someone else!), but in this book I am going to talk about money.

My motive is to help you personally. I know that most people live under some degree of financial pressure. That's why all of us can benefit from learning practical principles for managing our money better.

I have lived in America (for 10 years) and Australia (where I was born and now live), which are two of the richest countries in the world. Around ten percent of the world's population lives on just a few dollars a day. The majority of us are rich in comparison. Yet despite that fact, many people are under financial strain. Even a recent survey of Christians concerning their major pressures in life revealed that financial pressures were number one. People's average credit card debt is rising all the time and for many it is in the multiple thousands of dollars.

When we experience financial difficulties, every area of our life is affected. Churches often teach on giving but not enough about managing one's personal finances. It is a misconception to believe that giving alone guarantees financial freedom. It is only one part of the equation. There are many principles that must be consistently followed in order to become financially free.

When I was a teenager growing up in Portland, Oregon in the USA, my youth pastor (Wendell Smith) encouraged us to read one chapter from the book of Proverbs every day. I did this for quite a few years and I certainly gained a lot of wisdom for life through my reading and reflection. I learned about important matters such as the power of our words, the importance of diligent work, how to handle temptation, dealing with anger, keys to successful relationships and lots more.

Although the book of Proverbs was written thousands of years ago, it also has great wisdom for 21st Century people seeking to live wisely with the resources they have. This includes the fact that:

- Living with integrity is of greater importance than acquiring wealth.
- Hard work is the God-ordained way to generate income.
- It is foolish to try to get rich quickly.
- It is smart to avoid debt and to save for the future.
- Generous giving is to be commended and is often rewarded by God.

Following these general principles will usually lead to a blessed and prosperous life that enables a person to be a blessing to other people.

C. S. Lewis once wrote about an attitude he identified as "chronological snobbery" which is the belief that what is new is better than that which is old. Sometimes the new is better but not always. In fact, often ancient wisdom has proven itself to be reliable and has been tested by the sands of time. After all, there is really nothing new under the sun.

Yes, there are many excellent books, seminars and training courses about money today. I have learnt from many of them and I encourage you to do so the same (see Appendix 6 for a list of recommended resources). However, in this book I will be referring to a lot of teaching not only from the book of Proverbs but also from other parts of the Bible, simply because I think it contains some of the greatest insights available for becoming financially free.

I have written this book primarily for followers of Jesus and for churches who believe in the relevance of God's Word to us today but the principles are applicable to everyone. As humans, regardless of our faith or beliefs about spirituality, we all share similar challenges in life, including in the area of our finances.

I am really excited to be able to share these money talks with you. We will journey together through a variety of topics, including a story about a crafty manager, a personal money makeover, ideas for acquiring money, the power of generosity, saving and investing for the future, spending wisely, debt reduction, and living within our means. In addition, there are some appendices at the back of the book about alleviating poverty, church finances, fundraising, the purpose of business, recommended resources for digging deeper, and some reflection and discussion questions.

As you apply the insights we will share together, I know you will discover a greater degree of financial freedom that will bring a new dimension of joy and peace into your life. Who knows what the overflow of that will be - to those around you and ultimately to the world we live in. That's my prayer for you.

Let's begin …

Mark Conner
April 2018

CHAPTER 1

POVERTY OR RICHES?

Take a moment to read the following proverb.

> *Proverbs 30:7-9. O God, I beg two favors from you; let me have them before I die. First, help me never to tell a lie. Second, give me neither poverty nor riches! Give me just enough to satisfy my needs. For if I grow rich, I may deny you and say, "Who is the Lord?" And if I am too poor, I may steal and thus insult God's holy name. NLT*

If you are like me, you have a lot of questions buzzing around your mind after reading a proverb such as this. Is the wise sage presenting some kind of middle-class ideal, some kind of an in-between space between vast wealth and extreme poverty? Should a person seek to become poor to avoid the negative power of money? What about prosperity? How much is enough? Does God want his people to be rich or poor? Is God a prosperity preacher? What is his will?

It is difficult to summarize the teaching of Proverbs in a way that adequately answers these important questions. However, it is clear that the book encourages an avoidance of the extremes of both wealth and poverty. Instead, there are a variety of lifestyles some where in-between that allow for the wise accumulation of wealth as well as generous giving, so long as ethical living is pursued and devotion to God.

You don't have to live very long to realize that there are many stereotypes that portray distorted views about both wealth and poverty. Here are a few of them that I have observed:

1. **"Rich people are ungodly - they have so much wealth, so something must be wrong."** The truth is

that a person can be godly and wealthy at the same time.

2. **"Poor people are spiritual - they have given their all for God."** The truth is that a person can be poor and not be a person of faith.

3. **"Rich people are okay - they are blessed, so God must be happy with them."** The truth is that wealth is not necessarily a sign of God's approval or blessing.

4. **"Poor people are lazy and bad - it is their own fault they are poor. They must not be serving God, otherwise they would be blessed."** The truth is that a person can be poor and right before God.

I believe that God does want us to have money, but he does not want money to have a hold of us. Riches can be a threat to our relationship with God. Money is not the problem. It is our attitude towards it. Money is essential for survival and the establishment of a functioning society. God is very interested in money matters. They are important to him. He is a generous God who wants to give good gifts to his people. The key issue is an individual's motives, priorities and values.

In his excellent book *Neither Poverty or Riches: A Biblical Theology of Possessions*, Craig Blomberg takes an in-depth look at all of the Bible's teaching about money and possessions. For the purpose of this chapter, let's simply overview what the Bible has to say about the dangers and also the benefits of wealth.

The Dangers of Wealth

On the negative side, the various authors of the Bible teach us that money can become like a monster that rules our life if we allow it to. Money can be addictive, deceptive and destructive, and it is only temporal. Take a moment to read the following timeless wisdom from the sacred Scriptures:

Ecclesiastes 5:10-16. Those who love money will never have enough. How absurd to think that wealth brings true happiness! The more you have, the more people come to help you spend it. So what is the advantage of wealth — except perhaps to watch it run through your fingers! People who work hard sleep well, whether they eat little or much. But the rich are always worrying and seldom get a good night's sleep. There is another serious problem I have seen in the world. Riches are sometimes hoarded to the harm of the saver, or they are put into risky investments that turn sour, and everything is lost. In the end, there is nothing left to pass on to one's children. People who live only for wealth come to the end of their lives as naked and empty-handed as on the day they were born. And this, too, is a very serious problem. As people come into this world, so they depart. All their hard work is for nothing. They have been working for the wind, and everything will be swept away. NLT

Matthew 13:22. The seed falling among the thorns refers to someone who hears the word, but the worries of this life and **the deceitfulness of wealth** *choke the word, making it unfruitful.*

Luke 12:13-21. Then someone called from the crowd, "Teacher, please tell my brother to divide our father's estate with me." Jesus replied, "Friend, who made me a judge over you to decide such things as that?" Then he said, **"Beware! Don't be greedy for what you don't have. Real life is not measured by how much we own."** *And he gave an illustration: "A rich man had a fertile farm that produced fine crops. In fact, his barns were full to overflowing. So he said, 'I know! I'll tear* down my barns and build bigger ones. Then I'll have room enough to store everything. And I'll sit back and say to myself, My friend, you have enough stored away for years to come. Now take it easy! Eat, drink, and be merry!' "But God said to him, 'You fool! You will die this very night. Then who will get it all?' "Yes, a person is a fool to store up earthly wealth but not have a rich relationship with God." NLT

1 Timothy 6:9-10. People who long to be rich fall into temptation and are trapped by many foolish and harmful desires that plunge them into ruin and destruction. For **the love of money is at the root of all kinds of evil.** And some people, craving money, have wandered from the faith and pierced themselves with many sorrows. NLT

I am sure you would agree with me that there is some incredibly relevant insight in what we just read about money and wealth. Money can be difficult to master and that is why the apostle Paul declared that the love of money is the root of all kinds of evil. If you don't control your money, it will control you and it has the potential to destroy you. That is why the biblical writers gave so many warnings about the dangers of wealth. By the way, you don't have to have money to love it. Both poor people and rich people can be lovers of money.

Back in May 2000, a local newspaper in Melbourne Australia reported the story of Angelo Maurice Patti, a pensioner who stole 1.8 million dollars in money from his bank's automatic teller machines (ATMs). He thought it was his lucky day when an ATM started spitting out $50 notes. Then another teller machine did the same thing, then another and another. One day he emptied two machines of $139,000. A glitch with his debit card allowed him to withdraw an endless supply of cash from machines at gaming venues – despite his account being $200 in the red.

Over eight months, the 38-year-old invalid pensioner withdrew $1.8 million – and he knew how to spend it. He went on a spending spree: almost $500,000 in a share portfolio, paid off his de facto wife's house mortgage, renovated their house, bought a new car, bought a Harley Davidson motorcycle (and never rode it), and gambled away large amounts of it.

Once he realised what his card could do, Angelo couldn't help himself and spent wildly for eight months. He wanted more and more. He never had enough - $10,000, $50,000, $100,000, $500,000, $1 million, it kept on going! Angelo wrongly believed that money would bring him happiness. He thought his money would last forever. In the end, all of this money destroyed Angelo. Yes, what he did was unethical and illegal, but it was his greed that led to his arrest. His withdrawals were not recorded on the bank's mainframe computer and did not appear against his bank account. As his withdrawals became more frequent, he cleared two cash dispensing machines in one day. That activity alone led to his discovery and subsequent arrest. What a vivid reminder of the destructive power of wealth!

The Benefits of Wealth

On the positive side, the biblical writers also teach us that money can be a blessing in our life. God desires to bless his people and he prospers us for a purpose. Money can meet our basic needs, provide for our enjoyment, and enable us to meet the needs of other people and resource God's work on the earth. Here is some more ancient wisdom well worth listening to:

> *Deuteronomy 8:10-15. When you have eaten and are satisfied, praise the LORD your God for the good land*

he has given you. Be careful that you do not forget the LORD your God, failing to observe his commands, his laws and his decrees that I am giving you this day. Otherwise, when you eat and are satisfied, when you build fine houses and settle down, and when your herds and flocks grow large and your silver and gold increase and all you have is multiplied, then your heart will become proud and you will forget the LORD your God, who brought you out of Egypt, out of the land of slavery.

Ecclesiastes 5:18-20. Even so, I have noticed one thing, at least, that is good. It is good for people to eat, drink, and enjoy their work under the sun during the short life God has given them, and to accept their lot in life. And **it is a good thing to receive wealth from God and the good health to enjoy it.** To enjoy your work and accept your lot in life – this is indeed a gift from God. God keeps such people so busy enjoying life that they take no time to brood over the past. NLT

1 Timothy 6:17-19. Tell those who are rich in this world not to be proud and not to trust in their money, which will soon be gone. But **their trust should be in the living God, who richly gives us all we need for our enjoyment.** Tell them to use their money to do good. They should be rich in good works and should give generously to those in need, always being ready to share with others whatever God has given them. By doing this they will be storing up their treasure as a good foundation for the future so that they may take hold of real life. NLT

Money is not bad in and of itself. In fact, it can be extremely useful in the hands of the right person. Money can buy things you need while lack of money can limit what we can do. There are a lot of things we cannot do because we don't have the money necessary to acquire or accomplish them.

Warren Buffet is an American business person who serves as chairman and CEO of Berkshire Hathaway. He is considered one of the most successful investors in the world and has a net worth of over $87 billion as of 17th February 2018, making him the third wealthiest person in the world. Yet he is known for his personal frugality despite his immense wealth. He is also a notable philanthropist, having pledged to give away 99 percent of his fortune to philanthropic causes, primarily via the Bill and Melinda Gates Foundation which seeks to enhance healthcare and reduce extreme poverty globally.

Most of us will never have the kind of wealth that Warren Buffett has but I believe that God wants to bless and prosper each one of us. In my mind, to truly prosper means to have your own needs met (not your greeds) and enough extra to give away. It means to have more than enough.

We should desire money for the right reasons. Money is not evil, the love of it is. God blesses us so that we can be a blessing to others and to our world. Life is about what you can give not what you can get. It is okay to be blessed with money but don't be ruled by it.

Now it's time for a story about a shrewd manager.

CHAPTER 2

A STORY ABOUT A SHREWD MANAGER

Jesus was a remarkable speaker who captivated audiences both large and small, sharing life-changing insights with them. When observing his communication style we note that he never taught without using a story or an illustration (Mark 4:34). One of his common teaching methods was the use of parables — stories used to teach practical principles for living. Let's take a look at one of Jesus' most intriguing parables as recorded in Luke 16:1-13.

> *Jesus told his disciples: "There was a rich man whose manager was accused of wasting his possessions. So he called him in and asked him, 'What is this I hear about you? Give an account of your management, because you cannot be manager any longer.'*
>
> *"The manager said to himself, 'What shall I do now? My master is taking away my job. I'm not strong enough to dig, and I'm ashamed to beg— I know what I'll do so that, when I lose my job here, people will welcome me into their houses.' "So he called in each one of his master's debtors. He asked the first, 'How much do you owe my master?' "'Nine hundred gallons of olive oil,' he replied. "The manager told him, 'Take your bill, sit down quickly, and make it four hundred and fifty.' "Then he asked the second, 'And how much do you owe?' "'A thousand bushels of wheat,' he replied. "He told him, 'Take your bill and make it eight hundred.'*
>
> *"The master commended the dishonest manager because he had acted shrewdly. For the people of this world are more shrewd in dealing with their own kind than are the people of the light. I tell you, use worldly*

wealth to gain friends for yourselves, so that when it is gone, you will be welcomed into eternal dwellings".

"Whoever can be trusted with very little can also be trusted with much, and whoever is dishonest with very little will also be dishonest with much. So if you have not been trustworthy in handling worldly wealth, who will trust you with true riches? And if you have not been trustworthy with someone else's property, who will give you property of your own?"

"No one can serve two masters. Either you will hate the one and love the other, or you will be devoted to the one and despise the other. You cannot serve both God and money." NLT

Your Money Matters

It is estimated that Jesus talked about money and possessions in 16 out of 38 parables and 1 out of every 10 verses in the Gospels refer to this topic. Surprisingly, Jesus talked more about possessions and money than about heaven and hell combined.

There are approximately 500 verses in the Bible on the subject of prayer, less than 500 verses on faith but over 2,000 verses about money and possessions. There are over 1,000 verses on money alone (second only to the subject of love). As you can see, the various authors of the books of Bible talk a lot about money because your money matters – to God and hopefully to you too.

Now back to Jesus' parable …

Interpreting the Parable

Let's unpack this parable and see what Jesus is trying to say.

Jesus is speaking directly to his disciples, not to the crowd or the religious leaders. The story starts with an initial interaction between a business owner (the master)

and his employee (the servant) then moves to the manager's interaction with some of his boss' creditors before finishing with a final interaction between the boss and this manager. Finally, we then have some closing comments and instructions from Jesus about the topic.

> *Vs.8. The master commended the dishonest manager because he had acted shrewdly.*

There is a difference of opinion as to what exactly Jesus is commending about the manager in the story. This person started out as dishonest and therefore lost his job. His subsequent actions could be interpreted in two ways:

1. He was doing another dishonest act to help himself financially. The master praises him for his cleverness and wise self-interest, which obviously worked for this former employee.

2. Or he was discounting the debts by removing his part of the commission, thereby acquiring some money for his boss while also gaining favour with the customers through the discounts he gave them. This would not be a dishonest act but would be a smart thing to do. [The text doesn't give us this information, but it is a possible explanation]

Either way, as Craig Blomberg articulates in his book *Interpreting the Parables* (Downers Grove, IL: InterVarsity Press, 1990), the application of the parable is very clear:

1. All of God's people will be called to give an account for how they have served him and what they have done with their resources.

2. Preparation for that day of account should involve the wise use of all of our resources, especially in the area of our finances.

3. Wise use of resources, demonstrating a life of true discipleship, will be rewarded with eternal life and joy.

Jesus then adds a few other lessons after he has finished with the story:

1. How we handle small things is an indicator of how we will handle larger things (vs.10). Faithfulness (and also dishonesty) begins with the little things.

2. God looks at how we manage the financial resources ('worldly wealth') he puts into our hands to determine how much spiritual responsibility ('true riches') he can give to us (vs.11). Money is a test of spiritual maturity. It reveals our heart and the quality of our character.

3. How we handle or manage other people's things is a test of our character and maturity (vs.12). If we cannot do well looking after what belongs to another person, we will probably not be given our own.

4. Finally, Jesus observes that you cannot serve God and money, in the sense of making an ultimate commitment to both at the same time. Obviously, Jesus is saying that a real test of our discipleship is our attitude towards and our management of our finances.

You can tell a lot about a person by how they spend their money. It is more than merely numbers. It reflects a person's true values and how they feel about a lot of matters. As part of another teaching about money, Jesus said, "Where your treasure is there your heart will be also" (Matthew 6:21). In other words, your money follows the desires and values of your heart.

Jesus also said that the children of this world are often wiser in how they handle their finances than the children of light (vs.8). This was not a compliment! It shouldn't be that way. We need to gain knowledge about how the financial world works. God wants us to have both *faith* (to trust and believe him) and *wisdom* (good common sense about how to live successfully) in the area of our finances.

We are accountable to God for how we spend our money. Money management is a part of being a follower of Jesus. Discipleship is holistic. It should impact every area of our life, including the management of our money. That is why these money talks are so important.

Next up, it's time for a Personal Money Makeover.

CHAPTER 3

YOUR PERSONAL MONEY MAKEOVER

Everyone is into makeovers today - whether the goal is to overhaul their garden, completely renovate their house or lose some weight. Why not engage in a Personal Money Makeover?

Any makeover begins with taking an accurate *assessment* of where you are at right now. It is about defining reality. We can do this by participating in a very simple *financial check up* or audit. [For some of you this will be somewhat new. For others it will be very basic. Of course, even if you know something you can learn something new or at least be reminded of it so you can ensure you are putting it into practice, as well as be empowered to help others]

This is what you need to know about your finances:

1. **What you Own - your Assets.** Assets are anything you own that has value - cash, a house, a car, furnishings, tools, investments, money owed to you, etc.

2. **What you Owe - your Liabilities or Debts.** Liabilities refer to what you owe to someone else - a personal loan, a bank loan or a credit card debt.

3. **What you Earn - your Income.** Income can include your wages or salary, investment returns, gifts or donations received, government support, a pension, royalties earned, etc.

4. **What you Spend it on - your Expenses.** Expenses include all your living expenses (accommodation, food, clothing, etc), loan or debt repayments, etc.

The first two items are the key components of a financial statement referred to as a *Balance Sheet*. Subtract what you owe (your liabilities) from what you own (your assets). Hopefully, you have a positive 'net worth' or 'equity'.

CNN Money has a helpful net worth calculator on their web site. It only takes 5 minutes to complete and it is worth doing an exercise such as this at least once per year. You can access it at: http://cgi.money.cnn.com/tools/networth/networth.html

With any *Balance Sheet* the percentages and proportions are more important than the actual dollar amounts. For instance, if you have assets of a million dollars and yet your liabilities are over a million dollars you could be experiencing more financial pressure than someone with total assets of only $50,000 but with liabilities of only $40,000.

The third and fourth items are the primary components of another important financial statement referred to as a *Profit and Loss Statement*. Subtract your expenses from your income. You can view this from a weekly, monthly or annual perspective. Hopefully, there is a profit because you are spending less than you are earning.

Again, with a *Profit and Loss Statement* the percentages and proportions are more important than the specific dollar amounts. For instance, if you are earning $100,000 a year but are spending $120,000 annually, you are in a much worse financial condition than someone earning $40,000 a year but only spending $35,000 annually.

Does doing an assessment such as this take time? Yes! Is it worth it? Definitely! Ask for some help if you need to. Make use of a simple computer program if you want to and even consider taking a basic accounting course in order to gain more understanding in financial matters. Remember, Jesus said that how we manage our financial resources is very important.

A *Balance Sheet* statement is essential as it is a snapshot of your current financial position at any given moment in time. However, it is simply a result of what you do on a day-to-day basis with your finances, which is revealed by your *Profit and Loss Statement*.

If you would like your assets to increase and your debts to decrease over time, then you need to ensure that your income is exceeding your expenses on a regular basis then apply the resulting profit to those goals.

This is a short and simple chapter but it is vitally important. **Managing your financial resources well requires having an accurate assessment of your current financial situation - what you own (assets), what you owe (debts), what you earn (income) and where it goes (expenses).**

When you stop to measure your physical weight, the scales don't lie and when you engage in this kind of Personal Money Makeover, the numbers don't lie either. Financial freedom begins with being brutally honest about your current situation. This is your starting point. See your situation for what it really is and then have the courage to change it. You have to know what you are dealing with before you can move forward with confidence.

Do you know this information? If so, great. You know where you are at and where you need to go. If not, why not get a handle on it right away. In fact, why not pause and do it now? Hop up on the scales and do an accurate assessment of your financial health. Make it your personal assignment. Don't put it off.

Your Personal Money Makeover

BALANCE SHEET	PROFIT AND LOSS STATEMENT
Assets -	Income -
Liabilities =	Expenses =
Net Worth	Profit or Loss

We will talk about the income and expense side of your finances shortly but first of all some more basics.

CHAPTER 4

THE POWER OF A BUDGET

If you want to be financially free, you need to take charge of your finances. If you don't take control of your money it will take control of you and your life. Money is a great servant but a cruel taskmaster.

A budget is an important and effective tool for bringing and keeping your finances under control. A budget is simply a plan for earning and spending money. It provides limits and boundaries, which give security. It protects us from indulgence spending yet provides freedom within it.

There are many insights about planning in the Bible. Here are a few of them, full of wisdom for our financial world today:

*Psalm 20:4. May he give you the desire of your heart and make all your **plans** succeed.*

*Proverbs 15:22. **Plans** fail for lack of counsel, but with many advisers they succeed.*

*Proverbs 16:3. Commit to the LORD whatever you do, and your **plans** will succeed.*

*Proverbs 21:5. **Good planning** and hard work lead to prosperity, but hasty shortcuts lead to poverty. NLT*

Proverbs 27:23-24. Be sure you know the condition of your flocks, give careful attention to your herds; for riches do not endure forever, and a crown is not secure for all generations.

*Jeremiah 29:11. For I know the **plans** I have for you, declares the LORD, plans to prosper you and not to harm you, **plans** to give you hope and a future.*

Luke 14:28-30. "Don't begin until you count the cost. For who would begin construction of a building without first calculating the cost to see if there is enough money to finish it? Otherwise, you might complete only the foundation before running out of money, and then everyone would laugh at you. They would say, 'There's the person who started that building and couldn't afford to finish it!'" NLT

Yes, even Jesus taught about the importance and power of having a budget. It provides you with a simple tool for reviewing progress towards your goals, for reviewing your spending, and for checking whether you are on track or not.

Every budget begins with an assessment of our *income*, how much we earn. Only when we know this can we determine what we have at our disposal to spend. We will talk about acquiring income in the next chapter of our money talks.

CHAPTER 5

INCOME - HOW TO ACQUIRE MONEY

So, how do we get money or access income? Human work or labour is the means by which we can best earn the money we need to live our lives. It is the key to the *earning side* of the financial equation.

In the beginning, God worked. Genesis shows us that the creation of the world was God's "work" (Genesis 2:1-3), undertaken over a seven day work period. Not only does God work, he finds delight and joy in his work. God then commissioned humans to carry on his work in paradise (Genesis 1:26-28; 2:15).

In his book *Every Good Endeavor: Connecting Your Work to God's Work* (New York, NY: Penguin Books, 2014), author Tim Keller says, "Work did not come in after a golden age of leisure. It was part of God's perfect design for human life, because we are made in God's image, and part of his glory and happiness is that he works, as does the Son of God, who said, 'My Father is always at work to this very day, and I too am working' (John 5:17)." Keller goes on to say, "Work is as much a basic human need as food, beauty, rest, friendship, prayer and sexuality ... without meaningful work we sense significant inner loss and emptiness ... we need work to thrive."

Work was not part of the curse after sin entered the world. Before the fall, humans were to tend and keep the garden God had placed them in.

> *Genesis 2:15. The LORD God took the man and put him in the Garden of Eden to work it and take care of it.*

This work included physical activities as well as mental work such as Adam's task of naming the animals (Genesis 2:20). After sin entered the world, humans were to continue to work the ground but with the added curse of thorns and thistles along with the sweat of man's effort (Genesis 3:19, 23). As a result, work can bring frustration apart from God and his purpose (see Ecclesiastes 4:4).

God gives to each one of us skills and abilities so that we can use them to serve others in exchange for income. Look at the following statement:

> *Deuteronomy 8:18. Remember the LORD your God, for it is* **he who gives you the ability to produce wealth**, *and so confirms his covenant, which he swore to your forefathers, as it is today.*

Notice that God does not give us money. Now, that would be nice, a little envelope full of cash on the front doorstep at the beginning of each day! But that is not the way the world works. What God does give us is the ability to produce wealth. He is in the power-giving business not the money-giving business.

God blesses our labour and good old fashioned hard work provides us with a financial income. Normal life includes earning your own living. Everyone should be working - doing some useful task and/or being involved in a profitable occupation.

The writers of the Old Testament praise hard work, while condemning and ridiculing the lazy person, often referred to as the "lazybones".

> *Proverbs 6:6-11. Take a lesson from the ants, you lazybones. Learn from their ways and become wise! Though they have no prince or governor or ruler to make them work, they labor hard all summer, gathering food for the winter. But you,* **lazybones**, *how long will you sleep? When will you wake up? A little extra sleep, a little more slumber, a little folding of the hands to rest – then poverty will pounce on you like a bandit; scarcity will attack you like an armed robber. NLT*

Proverbs 10:4. **Lazy people** *are soon poor; hard workers get rich. NLT*

Proverbs 13:4. **Lazy people** *want much but get little, but those who work hard will prosper. NLT*

Proverbs 14:23. Work brings profit, but mere talk leads to poverty! NLT

Proverbs 20:4. Those **too lazy** *to plow in the right season will have no food at the harvest. NLT*

Proverbs 21:25-26. Despite their desires, the **lazy** *will come to ruin, for their hands refuse to work. Some people are always greedy for more, but the godly love to give! NLT*

Proverbs 24:30-34. I walked by the field of a **lazy person**, *the vineyard of one with no common sense. I saw that it was overgrown with nettles. It was covered with weeds, and its walls were broken down. Then, as I looked and thought about it, I learned this lesson: A little extra sleep, a little more slumber, a little folding of the hands to rest – then poverty will pounce on you like a bandit; scarcity will attack you like an armed robber. NLT*

Proverbs 26:14. As a door swings back and forth on its hinges, so the **lazy perso**n *turns over in bed. NLT*

It is important to note that short pithy proverbs such as these are usually generalizations. No doubt there are many poor people who are lazy but there are also many others who are victims of circumstances beyond their control, due to the presence and problem of socio-economic injustice. Poverty can sometimes be affected by capitalism gone wrong and global greed.

Every prosperous person in the Bible was a diligent worker, without fail. Diligence usually brings wealth and profit. It can lead to personal satisfaction and promotion (Proverbs 13:4; 22:19). In contrast, laziness often results in poverty and scarcity. It can even lead to slavery and bondage. It never satisfies. That is why there are so many rebukes to the lazy person.

The same attitude about work is found in the New Testament. Jesus Christ's work was given to him by his Father and he was always about his father's business. His task was to train disciples, teach about God's kingdom, and accomplish redemption for humanity through his death on the cross (John 4:34; 5:36; 9:4; 17:4). About his delegated work, Jesus said, "It is finished." Jesus then told his followers to keep occupied until he returned. They were to do business or to get to work putting the world aright - with justice, peace and love.

Don't avoid work and rely on others to support you. The apostle Paul accepted hospitality but did not depend on other people for a living (1 Thessalonians 2:9). He and his associates worked and they expected other Christians to work and earn their own financial support (1 Corinthians 4:12; 9:6. Titus 3:14). During one season of his life he worked night and day so as to not be a burden on anyone. Let's read part of a letter he wrote to a community of people living in the city of Thessalonica.

> *2 Thessalonians 3:6-13. And now, dear brothers and sisters, we give you this command with the authority of our Lord Jesus Christ: Stay away from any Christian who lives in idleness and doesn't follow the tradition of hard work we gave you. For you know that you ought to follow our example. We were never lazy when we were with you. We never accepted food from anyone without paying for it. We worked hard day and night so that we would not be a burden to any of you. It wasn't that we didn't have the right to ask you to feed us, but we wanted to give you an example to follow. Even while we*

> were with you, we gave you this rule: "Whoever does not work should not eat." Yet we hear that some of you are living idle lives, refusing to work and wasting time meddling in other people's business. In the name of the Lord Jesus Christ, we appeal to such people – no, we command them: **Settle down and get to work. Earn your own living.** And I say to the rest of you, dear brothers and sisters, never get tired of doing good. NLT

There may be situations or seasons where for various reasons we cannot work and we have to be dependent on others for income, whether that is the government, our family, or our friends.

However, as we can see, the primary means of acquiring income is through work. Work is part of God's plan for our lives. He works and he wants us to work too. We are created to make a contribution and to add value to the world we live in. In return we receive finances or reward for our efforts.

Acquire income through work – not through asking for a handout or by sitting at home waiting for a check to arrive in the mail. Have a work mentality not a welfare mentality. Also, avoid gambling.

What about Gambling?

I live Australia and Australians are amongst the world's leading gamblers which is not something we should be proud of. Gambling has been an inherent part of Australian culture from the beginning of European settlement. Australia has more poker machines per person than any country in the world, excluding casino-tourism destinations such as Macau and Monaco. It has nearly 200,000 machines – one for every 114 people. This has led to substantial increases in the amounts of money being wagered and net losses and has produced a massive revenue stream for governments.

In 1972-73, Australians lost almost $500 million gambling, which was about 1.55 per cent of household disposable income (HDI). By 1999-2000 they were losing over $13 billion, or over $900 per head - almost three times as much as in 1972-73 in real terms and equivalent to about 3.5 per cent of HDI. By 2014-2015, Australians lost more money gambling per capita than any other country in the world. Data from global consultancy H2 Gambling Capital puts Australia's total gambling losses per resident adult at about $1,000 a year, the highest amount in the world.

Tim Costello from World Vision Australia commented, "The best that can be said about the latest national gambling statistics is that at least the 2014-15 growth rate of 7.7 per cent to $22.7 billion has slowed to an increase of 3.9 per cent." He went on to say, "But when you are the world's biggest gamblers and 40 per cent clear of the next country, Singapore, in per capita terms, it is nothing to celebrate."

More money is now spent by Australians on gambling than is spent on sporting activities or cultural and entertainment activities. As many people don't gamble at all, these statistics mean that a very substantial amount of money is gambled and lost each year by those who do gamble.

Other Western nations are following a similar trend when it comes to gambling, which is leading to an array of harmful effects including crime, addiction, and even bankruptcy. Problem gamblers are likely to have a major depressive disorder and children of problem gamblers are at higher risk for a number of behaviors including problem gambling, tobacco use, and drug use. An Australian study found that one in five suicidal patients had a gambling problem.

It is estimated that every person with a gambling problem affects at least seven other people. Gambling often leads to preoccupation with getting money, increased risk-taking, repeated attempts to stop, and lying and engaging in illegal actions in order to obtain more money for the habit. Gambling destroys relationships and can result in depression and even suicidal tendencies.

So is it worth buying a lotto ticket or having a flutter on the horses? Well, actually, the chances of winning the lottery are only one in seven million. You are more likely to be struck by lightning!

Personally, I believe that gambling is diametrically opposed to God's financial plan. God in his wisdom connects the acquisition of money to hard work. Through the discipline of daily work we build character, we mature and we develop personal skills. As we do that diligently, our income grows and we can handle it because we have grown in character and maturity. People who want something for nothing usually don't develop the character necessary to handle it wisely. This can be observed by considering what happens to a person after they win a lot of money through gambling. Usually within a short time, they are back to where they were before.

Avoid Get Rich Quick Schemes

Wisdom teaches us to avoid the pursuit of any activity that promises quick money. Greed and haste tend to go together and can cause a lot of damage in our lives if we are not careful. Many times in the Bible we are urged to avoid all types of get-rich-quick schemes. Here are some examples:

> *Proverbs 12:11. A hard worker has plenty of food, but a person who chases fantasies has no sense. NLT*

Proverbs 13:11. Wealth from get-rich-quick schemes quickly disappears; wealth from hard work grows over time. NLT

Proverbs 20:21. An inheritance obtained too early in life is not a blessing in the end. NLT

Proverbs 28:20-22. The trustworthy person will get a rich reward, but a person who wants quick riches will get into trouble. Showing partiality is never good, yet some will do wrong for a mere piece of bread. Greedy people try to get rich quick but don't realize they're headed for poverty. NLT

There are a plethora of schemes today that promise a quick buck. Unfortunately, they usually result in disappointment and financial loss. Often things that seem too good to be true really are too good to be true. We do well when we exercise wisdom and caution in all our financial dealings and seek to generate income through hard work and wise investments, not through get rich quick pursuits. As Richard J. Clifford says in his commentary on the book of Proverbs, "Careful and steady work is better than frantically chasing rainbows."

How You Work Matters

When it comes to work, don't sit around and wait for the perfect job. Go out and get 'a' job to start with. Once you are moving, doors of opportunity tend to open up and you can make adjustments and appropriate changes along your vocational journey as you gain more and more experience.

It's one thing to have a job and know God's purpose for our work. It's another thing to consider *how* we go about our work. God desires that we work with diligence, integrity and an excellent attitude. This attracts God's favour and makes the Gospel attractive to a watching world. We are to serve people with love, working as to the Lord.

Here are **four ways to work as if your work really matters**.

1. **Be diligent.** Whatever your job is, develop your skill and be excellent at what you do. Then go about your work with all your heart, doing your very best.

   Colossians 3:23-24. Work willingly at whatever you do, as though you were working for the Lord rather than for people. Remember that the Lord will give you an inheritance as your reward, and that the Master you are serving is Christ. NLT

   'Whatever' covers every job you can imagine. Go about it with all of your heart and to a standard God would be pleased with. This means putting in extra effort, going the 'extra mile' (Matthew 5:41), doing more than expected and going about our work with an excellence of quality and attitude.

   Would you like a promotion? Arrive a little early and work a little late every day, and always do you very best with a joyful attitude. Then continue to develop yourself. Improve your skills, learn new things and gain all the experience you can. These are the principles of promotion.

   Diligence outworks itself in practical ways such as: respecting your boss or supervisor, exceeding expectations, doing your best, taking responsibility for mistakes, sharing the credit, being a good team player, resolving conflicts quickly, improving yourself, and volunteering for extra assignments. Diligence attracts the blessing of God and the favor of people (Proverbs 12:24; 13:4). You gain credibility by adding value to your workplace, resulting in growing personal influence.

Advance your career by developing yourself. See yourself as self-employed and take responsibility for your own growth and development. God's gift to you is your potential. Your gift to back to him is what you do with it. Invest in and improve your talents. Keep growing.

NBA basketball coach Pat Riley once said, "Excellence is the gradual result of always striving to do better." If you keep growing, everything you do will also. There will always be a place for you. Don't try to get ahead of others. Simply focus on improving yourself. It is not about being *the* best but about doing *your* best. That takes time and continual effort over the long haul.

Here is a good question: "If your job was advertised today, would you get it?" Sadly, many people wouldn't. Trends today indicate that those who have the most secure jobs are those who constantly acquire new skills, learn to work in a team, accept change and work for the benefit of the organization rather than against it.

2. **Be a person of integrity.** Integrity means there is an integration between who we say we are and who we really are. Honesty pleases God and can be a powerful witness to others (Proverbs 20:23). Be wise in your relationships. Work hard, and not just when the boss is looking (Ephesians 6:5-9. Colossians 3:22-25). Employers, do what is just and fair when dealing with your employees (Colossians 4:1).

3. **Be loving.** God calls us to serve others in love (Galatians 5:13). Love, or how we serve and treat other people, is to be our priority as followers of Christ (John 13:34-35. 1 Corinthians 13), and this includes our workplace. Daniel Goleman's landmark studies about people who are successful in the workplace reveal that "emotional intelligence" (our ability to control our own

moods and to get along with a wide range of people) is twice as important as IQ (intelligence) and technical skill.

4. **Be a witness for Jesus Christ.** Our work provides us with an opportunity to mix with 'outsiders'. Live in a way that is attractive to them, then look for opportunities to share a meal, to share your story, to share your faith, and to share about the good news of Jesus Christ (Colossians 4:5-6. 1 Peter 3:15). Of course, this missional focus should never be an excuse for being lazy or doing shoddy work

There's More to Life than Work

As important as our work is, there is more to life than work.

First of all, you are not your job. It is interesting to note that when we meet other people, one of our first questions (especially for men) often is, "What do you *do* for a living?" It is easy to become what we do. In contrast, God desires our primary identity to be in *who we are* not *what we do*. What we do is to be an expression of who we are. God does not want our work to become an "idol" that becomes the source of our identity, security and significance, leading to greed and workaholism. It is helpful to reflect on why we do what we do and to inject some fresh meaning and purpose into our work, beyond just making a living, climbing the corporate ladder, and/or being 'successful'. God is far more interested in who we are becoming than what we are doing for Him.

Secondly, you need to rest. The Sabbath principle is as important today as it was when it was first given. It was made for our benefit (Mark 2:23-28). On the seventh day, God "rested" from his work of creation and declared the day "blessed" and "holy" (Genesis 2:1-3). This principle was then reinforced as the fourth commandment (Exodus

20:8-11) which forbids being 'lazy' (you must work if you are able) or becoming a 'workaholic' (someone who never stops or slows down). Both work and rest are ordained and blessed by God.

Sabbath was a day of rest for the Israelites and violating it was a serious offence (Exodus 31:14. Numbers 15:32-36). The Sabbath was a reminder to them that while they rested, the world still functioned, even without their involvement. It was a joyous holy day, a day of spiritual refreshment, prayer, contemplation and worship with the community of faith.

Today we no longer need to keep the literal Sabbath Day as Israel did (Romans 14:5; Galatians 4:10; Colossians 2:16). However, we can glean some very important lessons from the principle of the Sabbath Day for our lives today. We can and should reclaim Jesus' liberating view of the Sabbath as a 'gift from God' for our benefit and a time for 'doing good'. This includes making church gatherings a priority in our schedule (Acts 2:42-47. Hebrews 10:24-25), spending time reading and meditating on God's Word (Joshua 1:8. Psalm 1:1-2. 2 Timothy 3:16-17), creating special times for family and friends, ensuring we take adequate time for rest and relaxation, and investing time in reflection and contemplation (Luke 5:15-16. Mark 1:32-39; 6:45-46). Rested workers are the most productive. Managing our energy as well as our time is a key to effectiveness. This requires creating an appropriate rhythm of work and rest, of activity and recovery.

Finally, you need to balance work with the other aspects of our life. Work takes a significant portion of our time and can fill as much of our life as we allow it to. Family, friends and our home church are also vital aspects of our life. In his letter to the Ephesians, the apostle Paul spoke about the importance of managing our time (Ephesians 5:15-16), then went on to speak about the priority of family life, calling husbands to love their wives as Christ loved the church (Ephesians 5:21 - 6:4).

Work and life balance are important. Both workaholism and striving to be rich should be avoided. Andy Stanley, in his book *When Work and Family Collide: Keeping Your Job from Cheating Your Family*, notes that there is more work to do than we have time, so someone will be 'cheated'. Don't allow work to cause you to cheat God and your family. Create boundaries. Draw lines. Determine when enough is enough. There is great power in being content with the current level of provision God has given us and then living within our means, rather than continually striving for more (Philippians 4:10-13. 1Timothy 6:6-10).

A Good Day's Work

So if you want to earn money, God wants you to work for it. Yes, you can also get money working for you through activities such as savings and investments, which we will talk about shortly, but it all starts with acquiring money through good old fashioned hard work.

Are you working this week? All of us are, hopefully - unless you are injured, incapable or retired. Let's work with all our heart, adding value to our world and as a source of earning income - to meet our own needs and to benefit others. Give your calling and vocation the best you can give it. When we excel in our work, God is honored and we are blessed in the process.

CHAPTER 6

A PLAN FOR FINANCIAL FREEDOM

An important part of your Personal Money Makeover was knowing what you are *earning*. What money do you have coming in? This is the *income* side of your budget. Your annual income may not seem like much to you but if you do the math you will be shocked at how much money you will acquire over a lifetime.

Interestingly, income is often the one part of the financial equation that we have least control over. The size of your income can be influenced by your parent's economic status, your education and training, your talents, skills and gifts, where you live and what you like to do.

Also, increasing your income does not always result in higher savings. People with higher incomes pay higher income taxes and generally have much higher standards of living and expenses, so their savings rate may in fact be less than yours. The assumption that someone who earns more than you is in better financial shape is often incorrect.

It's not how much you make but how much you spend - what you are doing with the money you earn. That brings us to the second part of our budget which is your *expenses*.

Reality means that you cannot keep everything you earn. You need to pay taxes, you have living expenses, and you may have debt repayments. This means you will have to achieve all of your future goals with the money that is left over, as well as with your existing assets and their earnings.

That is why we need **a plan** for doing three things with our money - **Spending**, **Saving** (or Investing) and **Giving**.

Most people only do one thing with their money – that's spend it! In fact, many people not only spend *all* of their income, they spend *more* than their income and as a result they are drowning in an ever-enlarging pool of debt.

I would like to strongly encourage you to start with something like the **10-10-80 plan**. The numbers 10-10-80 stand for: **give 10%**, **save 10%** and then **spend 80% or less**. Here it is in diagram form. Over the next few chapters we will unpack this in detail. Stay with me.

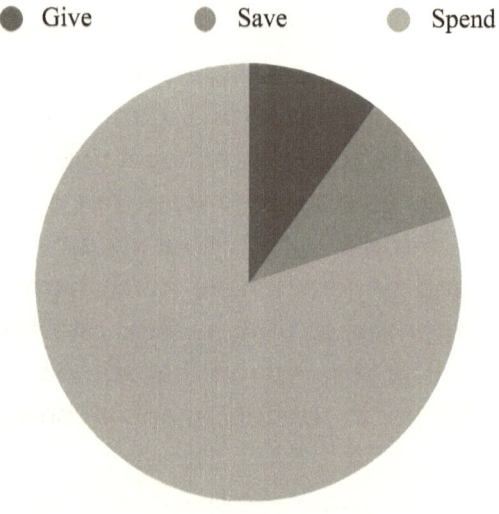

The 10-10-80 Plan

CHAPTER 7

GIVING - THE POWER OF GENEROSITY

"Make all you can, save all you can, give all you can."
John Wesley

First, give away 10% of your income. Pay it forward. That sounds crazy, doesn't it, but it is one of the unexpected keys to financial freedom. The happiest people on the planet are those who give. For Christians, I encourage them to give this first 10% to the local church they are a part of in order to resource the important work God is doing there. Some people refer to this as 'tithing', a biblical word that simply means a 'tenth'. This is a subject we will address in more depth in Appendix 3 on Church Finances.

For other people, I encourage them to give to specific individuals in need, to a good cause in their local community or to help meet a need in the broader world (see Appendix 2 about God's Heart for the Poor and Vulnerable). Pioneer philanthropist Andrew Carnegie was giving away 90% of his income near the end of his life.

I believe that God gives us our very breath and the power to acquire wealth. All that we have comes from him. He simply asks us to honor him by giving away the first part (not the leftovers) of all our increase. In doing so, we honor him as the source and owner of all of our resources. For people of faith, giving is an act of obedience and trust.

The Blessing of Giving

Jesus said and did many more things than what we have recorded in the four Gospels (see John 21:25). The apostle Paul gives us one of Jesus' non-canonical sayings when he quotes Jesus as having once said, "It is more blessed to give than to receive (Acts 20:35)."

Jesus is saying that when we give – whether it is our time, energy, service, encouragement, resource, or whatever – there is an even greater blessing than when we are on the receiving end. That sounds unnatural, almost counter-cultural, doesn't it. I mean, wouldn't we be happier if we were always on the receiving end of things? Well, even modern day psychological research, conducted by people such as Martin Seligman as reported in his book *Learned Optimism* (New York, NY: Random House, 1990), has proven that giving leads to longer and more lasting feelings of happiness and well-being than receiving does.

How is it more blessed to give than to receive? Here are three ways that I can think of:

1. God is Blessed When We Give

One thing we know for sure is that God is a generous God who gives so much to each of us, day after day. As we have already mentioned, he gives us the very breath that we breathe and life itself. He provides for our daily basic needs – food, clothing and shelter. He gives us the power and ability to get wealth. He is faithful in his love, mercy, and compassion towards us. He gave us his very best – his Son Jesus.

Not only is God a generous God in the very fabric of his nature, he also loves it when we are generous too. Generosity pleases him greatly. When we give we are just like him. He delights in us as his children when we take on his character qualities. Through generous giving we prove that God is first in our life and we honor him (see Deuteronomy 14:23. Proverbs 3:9). Paul tells us that God loves a cheerful (or joyful) giver (2 Corinthians 9:7). In contrast, selfishness, tightfistedness or stinginess displeases him because it is the exact opposite to his nature.

If you are a parent, have you ever had the experience of buying one of your kids a happy meal at McDonalds then later asking them for a few of their fries? How do you feel if they say, "No!" I tell you what I think, "Hey, I paid for those fries!" and, "I don't need your fries, I can buy all the fries I will ever need!" and "I can make sure you never have fries again while you live under my roof!" Again, I think those things, I don't say them!

I think that is how God must feel when we live stingy, tightfisted lives, refusing to share with others what is in our hand. After all, he is the fry maker! He can keep the fries coming or he can slow them down. When we live open-handed lives, giving generously of what is in our hand, God can flow more our way. This is the power of generosity.

God is blessed when his followers give because our generous giving helps his work on the earth to grow (2 Corinthians 9:11). God is honoured and his kingdom expands. The gospel is free but it takes resources (time, people and finance) to spread the good news, to build the church, to feed the poor and to create a better world. If everyone gave generously, according to their own resources and income, there would be more than enough for the work of each local church and every other good cause in society.

2. Other People are Blessed When We Give

We have all been on the receiving end of someone else's generosity. How does it make you feel? I think you would agree that it makes us feel special, valued and loved. Who doesn't love a thoughtful and generous birthday or Christmas present from a friend or family member.

When we give we have the opportunity to do the same for others. What a difference a gift can make. Other people are blessed in meaningful ways through our generous giving. God does some amazing things when his people embrace a spirit of generosity in every area of their life.

The church back in the first century experienced a powerful sense of God working amongst them which resulted in a tremendously positive impact on the local community, city and eventually the entire world of that time. An important factor in what God did was the generosity of Christians in contributing voluntarily, willingly and joyfully to what God was doing – and to the needs of others (see Acts 2:44-45; 4:32-37; 11:27-30; 24:17. Romans 15:25-28).

In my previous church, we established what we called a Barnabas Fund, named after Barnabas in the New Testament who gave of his resources so that vulnerable people could be helped (Acts 4:36-37). From this fund, we were able to help many people over the years with items such as car repairs, payment of phone and electricity bills, rent, rate payments, washing machines, medical bills, car insurance, gas bills, and various materials to renovate people's homes.

Here is a letter from one person who we were able to help:

"I lost my job last year. Then I had a nervous breakdown and couldn't work. Even though I got a casual job for 6 months this year, our family was really stretched financially. God provided to our needs in many amazing ways."

"One of the ways was our church offering us financial assistance. Because it's a caring church, the church leaders approached us through our small group leaders and offered to pay some bills we couldn't pay. That is love in action. When we were in need, the church was there for us, like in the book of Acts where the apostles

were serving the people. The heart of our church is about giving, about generosity. That's why we love it and we have no problem to give either. No wonder the church is growing and many individuals, many families are getting connected to this wonderful team who has the heart of God."

I love that. What a privilege we had to help people in this way. This was only possible because of the generosity of people giving to our church. Giving blesses other people.

Another woman in the church once spoke to me expressing how blessed her family had been by the generosity of the church. They had been in a tight time financially during which they received some financial assistance from the church. They also have a little boy who loved music and had evident musical gifting but they had not been able to afford an instrument for him other than a plastic guitar. During the singing time one day at a Sunday church service, the little boy was pretending to play the keyboard and a man in our church saw this. At the greeting time he came up to this woman and ended up giving her $300 to buy him a keyboard. This woman was beaming at how blessed she and her family had been by the generosity of someone else - actually a total stranger.

When we give we have the opportunity to do the same for others. What a difference a gift can make. Generosity is a sign of God's work in the heart of a person. Genuine spirituality touches not only the heart but also the wallet.

3. We are Blessed When We Give

This is the surprise element. When you give you receive! This is a powerful principle that often baffles the rational mind because it doesn't make sense.

Natural wisdom says, "When I give, I make a loss." God's wisdom says, "When you give, you actually gain!" This is the miracle of giving. When we give or invest in God's work it is not lost or gone. It is still there – in our heavenly investment account. God has a record of it and there is a multiplied return on what we give. Jesus teaches this, as does the apostle Paul. Take the time to read the following verses slowly.

Matthew 6:19-21. Don't store up treasures here on earth, where moths eat them and rust destroys them, and where thieves break in and steal. **Store your treasures in heaven**, *where moths and rust cannot destroy, and thieves do not break in and steal. Wherever your treasure is, there the desires of your heart will also be. NLT*

Philippians 4:10-19. I rejoiced greatly in the Lord that at last you renewed your concern for me. Indeed, you were concerned, but you had no opportunity to show it. I am not saying this because I am in need, for I have learned to be content whatever the circumstances. I know what it is to be in need, and I know what it is to have plenty. I have learned the secret of being content in any and every situation, whether well fed or hungry, whether living in plenty or in want. I can do all this through him who gives me strength.

Yet it was good of you to share in my troubles. Moreover, as you Philippians know, in the early days of your acquaintance with the gospel, when I set out from Macedonia, not one church shared with me in the matter of giving and receiving, except you only; for even when I was in Thessalonica, you sent me aid more than once when I was in need. **Not that I desire your gifts; what I desire is that more be credited to your account.** *I have received full payment and have more than enough. I am amply supplied, now that I have received from Epaphroditus the gifts you sent. They are* *a fragrant offering, an acceptable sacrifice, pleasing to God. And* **my God will meet all your needs according to the riches of his glory in Christ Jesus**.

1 Timothy 6:17-19. Teach those who are rich in this world not to be proud and not to trust in their money, which is so unreliable. Their trust should be in God, who richly gives us all we need for our enjoyment. Tell them to use their money to do good. They should be rich in good works and generous to those in need, always being ready to share with others. By doing this they will be **storing up their treasure as a good foundation for the future** *so that they may experience true life. NLT*

Where do you get a heavenly bank account? Which bank? Any time we do good and give to others, Jesus is indicating that we are storing up treasure in a heavenly account and it pays good returns. That's good news.

Paul is also using accounting language when he thanks the people in the church at Philippi for their donations. It is almost as if he is introducing something supernatural that takes us beyond simple 'double entry accounting', which only sees debits and credits, gains and losses. There is an added unseen dimension to every giving transaction. When you give you may have made a loss in the natural (a debit) while the recipient has made a gain (a credit) but there is also a deposit into your heavenly bank account that will pay good returns in due time. Welcome to 'triple entry accounting'!

Natural wisdom also says, "I will give when all my needs are met", "I cannot afford to give" or "I will give when I have some extra money." God's wisdom says, "Give now, even in your time of need, and watch me work!"

Isaac (Abraham's son) sowed crops in the land God had called him to and reaped a hundredfold return in a year of severe famine (Genesis 26:1, 12-14).

The widow who fed Elijah (1 Kings 17) was an unknown, unnamed single mother with one son. There was a famine in the land because of a drought. She and her son had been scraping things together for every meal. They only had a little left and they were about to have their last supper. The prophet Elijah, though powerfully used by God, was also a victim of this famine.

While staying as a guest at this woman's house, Elijah asked her to feed him first and if she did, God would re-supply the flour and the oil so she would have enough food for the future. Think about this – you are the woman and you are about to die of starvation. Elijah the prophet comes to the door and asks you to cook up your last ingredients into a meal for him. Is the promise of re-supply for this widow and her son going to come true? If not, they die now. If so, they have a future. By the way, imagine the local newspaper report - 'Traveling preacher eats widow's last meal!'

The woman did what she had been asked to do and a miracle took place. The oil lasted until the famine ended, feeding this single mother, her boy and the prophet.

If you give, will there be a re-supply? When God prompts you to give, do you trust his ability to give a return on your investment? Have you ever put yourself in a position to receive the miracle of re-supply? There is a certain type of spiritual growth that only comes through the adventure of this kind of giving.

Luke tells us about another widow (Luke 21:1-4). Jesus was sitting near the Temple treasury. The wealthy wanted to impress people and make a big deal out of their giving. This woman was not looking for attention and walked away humbly after giving her sacrificial offering.

Small gifts given in the right spirit really matter. Big gifts are fine but often they are given by people whose lifestyle is unaffected by a large gift and whose spiritual life is not expanded through entering uncharted waters. Large gifts can come from small hearts. On the other hand, small gifts can be big in God's sight.

Do you have no or little money? There is a temptation not to give. Why not trim somewhere and make a widow's small gift. It will touch the heart of God. Don't give destructively or irresponsibly. Obey God's prompting. He will lead you. Claim the promise of re-supply. God will be faithful.

Paul tells us that the churches in the region of Macedonia gave generously to the needs of others even during their own financial difficulty.

> *2 Corinthians 8:1-7. And now, brothers, we want you to know about the grace that God has given the Macedonian churches.* **Out of the most severe trial, their overflowing joy and their extreme poverty welled up in rich generosity. For I testify that they gave as much as they were able, and even beyond their ability.** *Entirely on their own, they urgently pleaded with us for the privilege of sharing in this service to the saints. And they did not do as we expected, but they gave themselves first to the Lord and then to us in keeping with God's will. So we urged Titus, since he had earlier made a beginning, to bring also to completion this act of grace on your part. But just as you excel in everything-in faith, in speech, in knowledge, in complete earnestness and in your love for us-see that you also excel in this grace of giving.*

When we are experiencing tough times financially, sometimes it seems easier to stop giving rather than to trust God. Yet when we give in faith (trusting totally in God) even when we are in a time of need, his miraculous provision begins to come our way. He only asks us to give of what we already have (not what we don't have) and as we go first, in faith and obedience, we release his blessing into our life. This principle is taught explicitly throughout the Bible and there are also many illustrations of people who experienced the miracle of giving and then God breaking through to meet their need.

Generosity has nothing to do with the amount given. It has everything to do with the attitude in which something is given. The Bible has much to say about the blessings that come through generous giving (see Psalm 112:5. Proverbs 3:9-10; 11:24-25; 19:17. Luke 6:38. 2 Corinthians 9:6). There is also a multiplication principle at work too. We reap more than we sow. The more we give the more returns usually come our way.

When we give we are blessed. Again, this should not be our *motive* in giving but it should be our *expectation*. We give because we *want to* and love to, not because we *have to*. As a by-product, we receive in the process. If you sow, you will reap. If you don't sow, you won't reap. This is a law and a principle that God has established. Giving requires this kind of faith.

Promises to the Generous

Take some time to read and think about these amazing promises to those who choose to be generous givers:

*Psalm 112:5. Good will come to those who are **generous** and lend freely, who conduct their affairs with justice.*

Proverbs 3:9-10. Honour the LORD with your wealth, with the first fruits of all your crops; Then your barns will be filled to overflowing, and your vats will brim over with new wine.

Proverbs 11:24-25. One person gives freely, yet gains even more; another withholds unduly, but comes to *poverty. A **generous person** will prosper; whoever refreshes others will be refreshed.*

*Proverbs 22:9. The **generous** will themselves be blessed, for they share their food with the poor.*

Luke 6:38. Give, and it will be given to you. A good measure, pressed down, shaken together and running over, will be poured into your lap. For with the measure you use, it will be measured to you. NLT

*Acts 10:1-6. At Caesarea there was a man named Cornelius, a centurion in what was known as the Italian Regiment. He and all his family were devout and God-fearing; he **gave generously** to those in need and prayed to God regularly. One day at about three in the afternoon he had a vision. He distinctly saw an angel of God, who came to him and said, "Cornelius!" Cornelius stared at him in fear. "What is it, Lord?" he asked. The angel answered, "Your prayers and gifts to the poor have come up as a memorial offering before God. Now send men to Joppa to bring back a man named Simon who is called Peter. He is staying with Simon the tanner, whose house is by the sea."*

*2 Corinthians 9:6. Remember this: Whoever sows sparingly will also reap sparingly, and **whoever sows generously will also reap generously**.*

Note that giving usually *precedes* God's blessing. "Honour the LORD with your wealth, with the first fruits of all your crops; *Then* your barns will be filled to overflowing …" It does not say, *when* your barns are filled with plenty, honour the Lord. Generous giving is usually the key to further financial blessing, not the result of it. Wisdom teaches us not to wait until we have a lot of money to start giving, but to give now of what we already have.

Stories of Financial Blessing

Does this really work? Today? Yes! Here are a few testimonies of people who have experienced the blessing that comes from giving generously.

A woman by the name of Sue began excitedly giving the weekly amount she had pledged to our church's building project. She had been struggling with poor health and required a few thousand dollars for treatment. Because she was only working part time and caring for her grandfather too, she thought about cutting back her commitment. However, she decided to push through. After this, she was given a computer and a visit from an IT expert to set it up. She also received an unexpected tax check which more than covered her health bills.

A man named Robert and his wife's income was stretched to the limit but they really wanted to contribute towards our church's fundraising project. They made a pledge in faith and in addition participated in two mission trips. Before these pledges were due, Robert unexpectedly received a letter from SHELL telling him that they had made 3,000 wrong transactions on his fuel card over a number of years resulting in over $8,000 in refunds.

Another couple in the church gave the monies set aside for an overseas holiday they had dreamt of and saved for over a number of years. Later that same year they received an unexpected inheritance that more than covered the costs of the holiday they thought they may not have been able to ever take.

My wife and I made a two year pledge back in 2002 to our local church's building expansion. We knew it would be a big stretch for us. Back in 2001, we had purchased a home on the outskirts of the city we lived in as a place for Nicole's parents (who had recently moved down from Queensland) to live and also as an investment property for us. At the time we purchased the home the capital growth rate in that suburb was 5% per year.

As it turned out, Nicole's parents loved the area but found Victoria a little too cold for them so they decided to move back to Queensland. As a result, we placed the property on the market. We sold it in December 2003, two years after we purchased it and we made an 80% profit over the two year period we had owned the property. That was 40% growth for two years in a row. The amount of the profit covered our entire commitment plus about 60% extra - all in one single transaction.

We also ended up selling our own home at the top of the market and we managed to build a new home at a very reasonable price. All of this occurred during our largest ever financial commitment, something we would have never dreamed possible. All this to say - we are not the smartest property investors, that's for sure!

It is important to note that generous giving is not some magic formula that will automatically solve all of your financial problems. If you have not been managing your finances wisely and you are in huge debt, you will need to make some changes to the way you are living and handling your resources. Giving is not some quick fix solution but it does set us on the path to financial freedom. In fact, there is often a delay between what and when we sow and when we reap. It is usually not immediate.

The apostle Paul put it this way:

Galatians 6:9. Let's not get tired of doing what is good. At just the right time we will reap a harvest of blessing if we don't give up. NLT

Giving financially is one way of 'doing good'. With our generosity there is a promise of reward or of reaping a harvest but there is a need for patience and perseverance.

The right time may be later than we think and may even be in the next life (1 Timothy 6:17-19). However, generosity pleases God and is eventually rewarded.

The Generosity Factor

Without God's help we will easily succumb to materialism, become prisoners to our debt, and be unable to experience the joy of generous giving. With God's help we can curb the spirit of greed that so pervades our society, live within our means, and have a generous spirit of giving. God blesses us not just as an end in itself (though he delights in this) but so that we can be a blessing to others.

The truth is that God can make your 90% go further than we can make our 100% go without his help and blessing. Giving is the *faith* side of our financial management.

Are you experiencing the generosity factor in your life? How would you describe yourself? If you are not yet a giver, why not step out and begin today. Don't live your life only on the receiving end and never on the giving end. That's not the highest level of living. Yes, there are times when we are in this position, maybe because of the circumstances of life, but we don't have to stay here. We can choose to move over to the giving side of the equation, even if it's small to start with. May others benefit because of your life. Make a difference by making a contribution.

If you are already an occasional giver, fantastic. Keep doing good. Stretch a little more. Become a regular and a generous giver. When we do our part with what is in our hand, God does his part. Jesus fed 5,000 people with a little boy's lunch. What is in your hand? God can do miracles through our little when we place it in his hand.

If you are a generous giver, thank you for the difference you are making already. This is an exciting topic for you. Another message on giving! We tend to get excited about the things we are passionate about and where our heart is.

Now let's move on to the *wisdom* aspect of our financial management. Remember, we need *faith* to please God and *wisdom* to make good daily choices.

CHAPTER 8

SAVING AND INVESTING - PREPARING FOR THE FUTURE

The next step in our financial management plan is to take another 10% and pay yourself by putting this in a savings or investment account. That's right, make a decision to pay two entities generously and consistently every time you receive any type of income - God and yourself.

Prepare for the future by crafting a savings and investment plan. Listen to some more wisdom from Proverbs:

> *Proverbs 21:20. The wise* **store up** *choice food and olive oil, but fools gulp theirs down.*

> *Proverbs 21:20. The wise person* **saves** *for the future, but the foolish person spends whatever they get. TLB*

What an incredible statement, written so long ago. Wise people store up or save for the future. Foolish people spend everything they have. If that doesn't speak powerfully into the very heart of our consumeristic culture today, I'm not sure what else does. **The number one money problem today is that many people spend more than they earn and as a result are going further into destructive debt.** It's time to get smart and change the equation.

Make a decision to become a saver and create a plan to make it a reality. Here is some more good advice worth heeding:

> *Proverbs 13:11. Dishonest money dwindles away, but whoever gathers money little by little makes it grow.*

> *Proverbs 13:11. Wealth from get-rich-quick schemes quickly disappears; wealth from hard work grows. NLT*

Imagine the difference it would make if we could simply spend less than we earn on a consistent basis, then save and invest the difference over a long period of time. That is what I call financial freedom. It's as simple as that.

Think about the **ants**. They are members of the animal kingdom with some of the smallest bodies and tiniest brains around but they are very smart. They store up (save) for the winter months (an economic downturn in Antsylvania!). We humans have bigger bodies and larger brains but sometimes we are pretty foolish. We have nothing saved up for the future.

> *Proverbs 6:6-11. Take a lesson from the ants, you lazybones. Learn from their ways and be wise! Even though they have no prince, governor, or ruler to make them work, they labour hard all summer, gathering food for the winter. But you, lazybones, how long will you sleep? When will you wake up? I want you to learn this lesson: A little extra sleep, a little more slumber, a little folding of the hands to rest – and poverty will pounce on you like a bandit; scarcity will attack you like an armed robber. NLT*

Growth financially requires time and continued effort. Progress is step by step. It requires consistency - doing well for the long haul not just quick bursts of enthusiasm. If we are faithful with what we have, looking after it well, we prepare ourselves to receive more. Faithfulness is rewarded. Note Jesus' parables that include this statement - "Well done, good and faithful servant" (e.g. Matthew 25:21).

Are you ruling well over what you have now? Looking for more without handling what we already have is a sign of immaturity. God looks at how well we take care of what we have now to determine what we can receive in the future.

By taking 10% of your income and saving it for the future you tap into the power of compound interest for a good investment return. Albert Einstein once called compound interest the 8th wonder of the world. Its when you re-invest your income so you earn interest on your interest.

> Matthew 25:26-27. His master replied, "You wicked, lazy servant! So you knew that I harvest where I have not sown and gather where I have not scattered seed? Well then, you should have put my money on deposit with the bankers, so that when I returned I would have **received it back with interest**."

Saving is making provision for tomorrow. When we have savings that we have set aside we are prepared to handle emergencies that may come our way and we are also in a place to help others who may be in need.

We commend the Good Samaritan for his compassion but it is easy to forget that he was also empowered to help the man in need because he had managed his resources well. He had his own donkey, some oil and wine, and money to pay for a few night's accommodation and expenses. Because he had saved, he was able to give and help the vulnerable (Luke 10:30-35). When we don't have any savings we are easily shaken by emergency situations and we are not in a position to help others in need, even though we may want to do so.

How to be a Saver

Make a decision to be a saver. Start small if necessary but start. It will be worth it. Do you think you can't afford to save? Why not buy second hand goods instead of new ones or make your lunch rather than buying it. Buy goods during end of season sales rather than paying full price. There are many ways such as this to reduce your spending so you can be a saver.

Put together a savings plan. Make it automatic month after month. Do it direct if you can, using a payroll deduction for example. Don't leave cash laying around. Put your money into an investment account or fund before you use it. Set up a separate bank account with a high paying interest rate for your savings. Go for a zero fee account. Change banks, if necessary. Or increase your mortgage or superannuation payments. If you fail to plan, you plan to fail.

Save little and save often. No matter how small the percentage is, begin doing it now. Avoid the biggest enemy of saving - procrastination.

Find some help, if you need it. Choose an accountability partner. Obtain some good financial counsel. It is a worthwhile investment. Read books, listen to podcasts, attend seminars, and listen to sound advice from experienced investors.

Don't give up. A commitment to regular savings is vital. Persistence, discipline and time will work wonders for you. Simply save a few dollars a day year after year and you will be surprised how much your money will grow.

Be a steady plodder when it comes to saving. **Spend less than you earn, then save and invest the difference over a long period of time.** The key is time, not the amount. Save regularly and do it for a long time - and you will amass more than you can imagine.

Investments - Putting Your Money to Work

The *income* side of our financial equation is about working for money. The *investment* side is about getting your hard earned money to work for you - where it earns a profit. This is where we collect interest, dividends or returns, rather than pay them.

All investments involve a certain amount of *risk*, in the same way that life itself is not free of risk. Generally speaking, the greater the potential return the greater the possible risk.

There are a plethora of shonky investment schemes out there that promise you a fast track to wealth. If it sounds too good to be true, it probably is. Here is some more ancient wisdom, as relevant today as it was when it was first written:

> *Ecclesiastes 5:13-14. There is another serious problem I have seen in the world. Riches are sometimes hoarded to the harm of the saver, or they are put into* **risky investments** *that turn sour, and everything is lost. In the end, there is nothing left to pass on to one's children. NLT*

How true is that! Be careful about high-risk investments. Beware of investments that:

1. You don't understand. An old saying goes like this, "When a person with money meets a person with experience one ends up with the money and one ends up with the experience."
2. Have a high probability of loss.
3. Require an immediate decision to invest. Sleep on it. It will most likely still be available tomorrow.
4. Offer attractive tax incentives. Structure your investments to make money, not simply avoid tax.
5. Require little or no effort on your part.
6. Are offered over the telephone or through the mail. Beware of total strangers whose trustworthiness is not known.

7. Promise to make a large profit quickly. Again, if it sounds too good to be true - it probably is.

In the early 1990s, Nicole and I purchased our first investment property through the advice of a 'friend'. It was an 'off the plan' apartment in one of Melbourne's inner suburbs, which included saving significant stamp duty on the purchase. The trouble was we really didn't fully understand what we were getting ourselves into and we failed to read the fine print. In the second year, a lift maintenance levy of $8,000 per annum kicked in, which was a huge amount back then. A few years later, we managed to sell the apartment and just get our money back, although we lost a few thousand dollars on the transaction fees. It took us a few years to recover from this but we sured learnt a lot - the hard way!

Of course, there are many investments that can yield good returns. Do your research, acquire good advice and learn about different investment types - both their potential returns and risks.

There is also wisdom in diversifying your investments.

Ecclesiastes 11:2. Divide your investments among many places, for you do not know what risks might lie ahead. NLT

Some of the types of investments you may want to consider over time include:

1. Savings, which at least brings a minimal interest return.
2. Property, whether it be residential or commercial.
3. Shares, stocks or managed funds, which are ways to buy part ownership in a company or group of businesses. Consider re-investing your dividends for exponential returns over the long haul.
4. Establishing your own business.

5. Developing your vocational skills. This often increases your earning potential.

The number one investment for most people is to eventually own their home. Many people take out a 30 year loan and then pay it off in less time, say 15 years, by making extra and/or more frequent payments, and thereby saving large amounts of interest.

Your Future Goals

Planning or preparing for the future ahead of time is very important. In fact, planning is encouraged frequently throughout the Bible (see Psalm 20:4. Proverbs 15:22; 16:3; 20:18; 21:5; 27:23-24. Jeremiah 29:11. Luke 14:28). God gave Joseph a 14 year plan - 7 years of abundance followed by 7 years of famine that he was to prepare for (see Genesis 41). Think about it, God has Joseph thinking 14 years ahead! What a terrific example for us. We are not to worry about tomorrow but we are to prepare for it.

Proverbs 21:5. **Good planning** *and hard work lead to prosperity, but hasty shortcuts lead to poverty. NLT*

Proverbs 21:5. **Steady plodding** *brings prosperity; hasty speculation brings poverty. TLB*

What are your long term financial goals? What are some things you would like to do in the future that will require money? Writing them down will increase your ability and will-power to achieve them. It also gives you a motivation to save and invest your money in order to make them a reality. Nothing significant happens without preparation and that includes financial preparation.

Have you considered these things?

1. **Housing** - where you want to live and whether you will rent or buy (don't forget house and contents insurance

if you choose to purchase a home). Also, consider possible home renovations.
2. **Education** - for yourself and any children you may have.
3. **Holidays** you may want to take.
4. A **mission trip** you may want to go on.
5. Upgrading or changing over your **vehicle**. When it comes to choosing a vehicle, it's far better to buy something you can afford with cash than to take out a high interest loan on a rapidly depreciating item.
6. **Retirement** - how much will you need to live on when you stop working full time? The average lifespan has doubled and in retirement your biggest risk is that you will outlive your savings. Planning your investment into and the growth of your retirement account or superannuation fund is vital. Preferably, select a simple balanced fund with low fees. I should note that work is good for you and makes you happier and less prone to depression. So plan on using your skills for useful work as long as you can, even if it is for a day or so a week or as a volunteer.
7. **Disability** - ensuring your family is adequately cared for if you cannot earn an income. When it comes to matters such as insurance, it is important to balance *faith* (trust in God) with *wisdom* (preparing adequately for possible risk). Consider different types of insurance, including health, life and permanent disability. It is estimated that less than half of Americans have the right amount of insurance.
8. **Death** - ensuring your family is adequately cared for if and when your death occurs. The number of people who pass away without having a will and whose families are left with difficulties in managing an estate is quite staggering.

The Benefits of Saving

In the natural world, we plant seeds, we water them, we watch them grow, then in due time we reap a harvest. We can do the same with our money - plant seeds of savings and investment, watch them grow over time, then enjoy a harvest from the returns.

Sociological research reveals that, beyond a basic level of income (around $70,000 a year), there is no noticeable connection between a large bank account or a high income and happiness. However, what does have a measurable impact on happiness is savings. That's because savings equals freedom. When you have money in the bank, you have the power and the ability to live your life the way you want to because you don't owe anything to anybody. That's the power of savings.

The wise person understands these timeless principles and that's why they have a strategy for earning and saving, spending and giving. God is honoured, bills are paid on time, investments grow, and they are able to give generously on a regular basis.

The fool has no character, no plan and no discipline. They may feel free at the moment but they cannot handle an emergency and cannot give to the needs around them even if they want to. This often leads to financial pressure and anxiety.

Why save? Savings creates financial freedom, it reduces pressure, it eliminates worry and anxiety over financial matters, it enhances our joy, it can be an example to others, and it enables us to give when we feel prompted to.

In the next chapter we will talk about *spending* our money wisely.

CHAPTER 9

SPENDING - LIVING WITHIN YOUR MEANS

After *giving* 10% to God's work in the world and putting aside 10% into *savings* and/or investments, the final part of our strategy for becoming financially free is to endeavor to live on the remaining 80% of our income.

Use the remaining 80% or less to pay everyone and everything else. This is for all of your normal living *expenses* which are worth having specific budget allocations for - housing, food, clothing, transportation, debt reduction, entertainment, holidays, extra giving, etc. You have already honored God and paid yourself. You can now enjoy life a little because you are on plan. You are living wisely.

Beware of Budget Busters

Beware of major budget busters and especially 'impulse buying', which refers to unplanned expenditures that we make based on emotion. This is the number one budget buster. Some of us get excited at the very sight of the word 'SALE', an interest free offer or an offer of '2 for the price of 1'. Just because you can afford it doesn't mean you should buy it. If you buy something on sale, you are not saving, you are spending!

Research indicates that women do this more often than men. But men do it in larger amounts. Come on guys, that extra pair of shoes your wife recently purchased will not bust the budget as much as that new mega-size television you bought for the games room! In fact, when it comes to credit card debt, men owe an average of $450 more than women.

Advertising motivates us to buy things we often don't need and seeks to make us dissatisfied with what we have now. Advertising's aim is to tell you, "Last year's model is not good enough", "What you have now is not good enough any more" and "You need this!" It creates dissatisfaction.

The truth is that all material things always oversell themselves. They promise us satisfaction, prestige, power and security but rarely deliver on their promises over the long term.

Avoid situations that encourage you to spend, such as unnecessary visits to shopping center (some people go shopping when they feel depressed), watching too much television, store catalogues, and continual exposure to advertisements.

Be satisfied with what you have rather than focusing on what you don't have. Resist temptation. If you don't then pretty soon you can't honor God or pay yourself and you are living on 99% or more of your income.

Shopping Tips

Here are **some questions to ask yourself when considering a possible purchase:**

1. "Do I really need this?" There is no point buying something you don't need even if it is on sale for a good price.
2. "Is this a good price? Is it really a bargain? It is the current model? 40% off what?"
3. "Is this the best time for me to buy?"
4. "Do I really need a new one?" Buy second-hand, if possible.
5. "Have I done enough research?"

Here are a few **extra shopping tips** you might find helpful:

1. Take a shopping list with you. There is no benefit in wandering around shops and ending up buying things you had never even thought of purchasing beforehand.
2. Don't shop hungry. You will always end up buying more than you need.
3. Try to shop once a week at the most.
4. Consider shopping alone - without friends or family members.
5. Check the lower shelves, where items are often less expensive.
6. Understand unit pricing. Buy in bulk or quantity at bargain prices. Larger quantities are usually cheaper, but not always.
7. Avoid junk food - it is bad for you and often more expensive.

I remember early on in our marriage shopping for a new BBQ. The store had a sale on so I bought not only a whiz bang BBQ but also a heap of extras to go with it. In the end, I had overspent and busted our budget plans. It took a few months to recover from that impulse buying spree. Nowadays, when Nicole and I are discussing a possible purchase we will often say to each other, "Let's not do another BBQs galore!"

In addition to impulse buying, beware also of compulsive spending (spending because of a serious unmet need in your life), indulgence buying (buying things you don't need), boredom spending (having nothing to do so you go shopping), special interest spending (an area of weakness or an all-consuming hobby) and status spending (buying the latest and greatest stuff).

What about Debt?

Always do your best to pay your bills on time. Listen to this advice from the apostle Paul:

> *Romans 13:6-8. Pay your taxes, too, for these same reasons. For government workers need to be paid so they can keep on doing the work God intended them to do. Give to everyone what you owe them: Pay your taxes and import duties, and give respect and honour to all to whom it is due.* **Pay all your debts**, *except the debt of love for others. You can never finish paying that! If you love your neighbor, you will fulfill all the requirements of God's law. NLT*

Buying something on credit is a contract between the lender and borrower. It is an agreement to pay - it is deferred billing. IF you use credit cards wisely and always pay them off before the interest period begins you may benefit from them. If not, you will find yourself in trouble financially. It is estimated that the average American household has $16,061 of credit card debt. Far better to use cash or a direct debit facility if you are having difficulty with credit card debt.

Debt can put us under great pressure. If you are in debt, you must keep earning and as much as possible. Some people today end up working two jobs to earn enough to keep up with their debt repayments. This destroys their peace and their joy.

It is estimated that 40-50% of marriages today end in divorce. According to www.marriage.com, financial issues are the #2 cause of divorce, only surpassed by infidelity or extra-marital affairs.

Borrowing too much can reveal character flaws such as a lack of contentment, a lack of patience, a lack of self-discipline to say "No", and little self-control to refuse things we really don't need to have. As someone one said,

"Some people buy things they don't need with money they don't have to impress people they don't even like."

Because of this, it is wise to avoid all kinds of debt other than borrowing money for an appreciating asset such as taking out a mortgage for a home or acquiring a start-up loan for a good business opportunity. Always use debt wisely - to increase your net worth over time.

Ideally, the value of the item you purchase on loan should equal or exceed the amount owed against it both now and in the future. There must be enough equity for re-sale.

For example, a home loan is a debt but it is collateralized with the value of the house. You can exchange it at some time in the future, should you desire to do so. However, you cannot do this with most other acquisitions such as the clothes you have purchased or a holiday you have taken recently. You cannot sell those family photos for very much! Also, items such as a new car depreciate very quickly the moment a person drives out of the car yard.

A house loan is probably the best loan you will ever have. It usually includes low interest rates and is a good long-term investment. If you make occasional extra payments and/or pay every two weeks or even weekly rather than monthly, you will significantly reduce the term of your loan and save many thousands of dollars in interest in the process.

Ensure that any home loan payments are not so high as to strain your budget. Jesus said that the cares of the world and the deceitfulness of riches can choke us from a fruitful and joyful life (Luke 8:14). At times, we need to learn to show restraint and not pay too high a price for our acquisitions.

Avoid or at least reduce destructive debt. We are in trouble when we are spending more money than we are earning. Our society encourages us to go into debt and tries to make it as easy as possible. Low interest rate deals encourage people to borrow even more. Many stores offer long interest-free periods now if you buy through them (6 to 12 to 24 months and even longer). Learn to say, "No". Create some margin in your life. Simplify your life. Let love, joy and peace be your priority, not more stuff.

Warren Buffet, the greatest investor in history says, "Stay away from debt. If you're smart you don't need it. If your dumb you got no business using it."

Debt puts you in bondage, it creates stress, it puts you under pressure, it increases your risk, it can sabotage your peace and joy, it can damage your reputation, and it hinders you from being able to give. In many ways, debt is like slavery. It controls your life every single day.

Proverbs 22:7. The rich rule over the poor, and **the borrower is servant to the lender**.

Proverbs 23:4. Don't wear yourself out trying to get rich. Be wise enough to know when to quit. NLT

How to Get out of Debt

Every significant event in our life begins with a decision. Decide that you are going to be debt free and then begin to walk towards financial freedom. Choose life. You can do it.

Craft a plan for reducing and then totally eliminating your debt. Without doubt, it will require a change in your lifestyle. To clear your debts you will have to either earn more money and use that extra income for your debt reduction repayments OR you will need to reduce your expenses. That may sound hard but you can be happier and more content in the process.

Here are some tips to include in your debt reduction plan:

1. Prepare a new budget and then stay within its limits.
2. Don't take on any more debt from this moment on. Buy only with cash. Live simpler and happier. Be satisfied with what you have. Avoid situations that encourage you to spend. Know your weaknesses. Have a credit card meltdown party or cut them up and throw them away, if they are out of control.
3. List all of your creditors on a piece of paper then focus on paying off the debt with the highest interest first. Try to eliminate debt a soon as possible. Contact your creditors and express your intention to pay, asking for a lower interest rate and communicating to them your payment plan. Another option is to pay off your smallest debt first, simply to build some personal confidence and create some momentum in your debt reduction project.
4. Make a list of everything you own - all of your assets. Sell anything that is not really needed and use the proceeds to pay off some of your debt immediately.
5. Apply any additional income or cash to existing debts - not to new purchases.
6. If you are stuck, ask for some help, especially good financial advice. Consider making an appointment to see a reputable financial counsellor. It will be worth it.
7. Find an accountability partner. Someone cheering you on makes it easier to achieve your objective.

Don't give up. It took you time to get into debt and it will take you time to get out. But it will be worth it. Stay focused on the goal - being debt free.

Still Can't Make it Work?

Some of you may be thinking that living on 80% of your income is unrealistic. I honestly don't think it is. Scott Pape, author of the best-selling book *The Barefoot Investor*, recommends that living off even 60% of your income is an achievable goal for everyone, leaving the remaining 40% for savings, emergencies, debt repayment, investment and philanthropic giving. However, if you honestly can't live on 80% of your income you will have to make some changes for this plan to work for you. Essentially, you have two options.

First, you could earn some extra income by finding a higher paying job (upgrade your skills if necessary to make yourself more qualified) or working extra hours at your current job or starting an additional job (possibly part time). These are all possible options but consider the ramifications of each choice.

We should seek to avoid the extremes of working too little or working too much and becoming a workaholic. Where are you on the continuum right now? Which way do you need to move? Is it time to get off the couch or time to slow down a little? Do you have a job or a life? Are you obsessed with working and earning more money? Sometimes, less is actually more.

The second option is to reduce your expenses. This is really your only other option and it may require you to down-size your living standards. On this matter, the wisdom from the sacred text calls to us once again:

> *Ecclesiastes 4:6. Better to have one handful with quietness than two handfuls with hard work and chasing the wind. NLT*

Think about that. Could it be better for you to have *less* and with it joy and peace than to have *more* and the debt and accompanying stress that goes with it? I believe so.

If your standard of living is creating pressure and anxiety in your life and relationships, why not lower it? Right-size your living expenses to match your income.

I will never forget meeting a married couple after a church service one day where I had taught some of these principles of wise financial management. The woman's husband was visiting church for the first time and was not a Christian. Instead of being upset that I had spoken about money (!) they shared about the financial pressure they were both under and how my message had spoken right into their situation. At the time, they were living in such a large house that they both had to work full time just to pay their mortgage, which was creating all sorts of conflict in their relationship. I prayed with them and encouraged them to seriously consider down-sizing.

A few months later, they came and saw me. There were smiles all around. Not only had the husband become a Christian during that time and started coming to church regularly, they had sold their house and bought something smaller. The woman was now working only part time and they were about to start a family. Money cannot buy the kind of joy and peace they had found. Less can really be more.

America has one of the highest rates of household debt in the world mainly due to out of control spending. Americans also on average live in some of the biggest homes in the world. Why? Because we need room to store all of our stuff. No wonder the self-storage business is booming! How much is enough? Is our uncontrolled accumulation of more stuff making us happier or simply adding more stress into our lives?

Interestingly, we often think that wealthy people have high incomes, live in wealthy suburbs with huge homes and drive expensive cars. However, a research study reported in the book *The Millionaire Next Door* revealed that these kinds of people are often asset poor and are drowning in debt. In contrast, the genuinely wealthy usually live in modest homes in average suburbs, are long term investors, avoid credit cards, and drive second hand family cars.

Unfortunately, most people think that the solution to their financial problems is to earn more money. This is not true because chances are they will overspend any extra income they receive anyway. The solution is to cut back on expenses so you are spending less than what you earn. It really is not what you earn that matters most – it is how much you spend.

I will say it again: **if you consistently spend less than you earn and save or invest the balance, you will gain financial freedom.** It has nothing to do with *how much* you earn. Overspend by a few dollars a day and you can be thousands of dollars in debt in a number of years. On the other hand, put aside a few dollars a day into savings and you will save thousands of dollars in a number of years.

Most financial problems or difficulties occur because of improper spending of money. Many people spend all that they earn, living well beyond their basic needs (food, shelter and clothes) and spending money on things they want rather than what they really we need.

The Seasons of Life

Life has different seasons and our financial situation varies within them. Let's look at a few of them.

1. **Single**. You should be able to give and save quite a fair amount of your money at this time of your life if you control your spending. Save and invest in the future. I had saved over $10,000 before Nicole and I were married back in 1985. Many friends my age at the time

earned as much as I did and even more but simply spent it all.
2. **Married without Children.** If you both work, you also have the opportunity to give and save quite a lot of money. Prepare for the future. Save and invest wisely.
3. **Married with Young Children at Home.** Life gets a little more expensive now . There are more expenses and usually one partner spends more of their time at home.
4. **Married with Children in School.** This can also be an expensive time of life with education expenses, clothes, to buy and food for growing teenagers. Unless one spouse is on a fairly high salary, it is highly likely that the other spouse will need to work also, maybe part time, to cover the kind of expenses you will most likely have with items such as buying a house and raising a family. Saving may be a little more difficult during this season.
5. **Single parents** have extra challenges, including financially. This is where extended families and a church community can be a great support.
6. **Empty Nesters.** As your children grow up and leave school and find their own jobs expenses can ease off a little and the potential of saving more emerges.

The lesson is to maximise the times when there is more so you are prepared for the times when there is less. Again, this is the Joseph Principle - saving during times of abundance so you have enough during times when things are tight.

Next, it's time to wrap things up before we share some extra material for those interested in the issue of poverty, in church finances, in fundraising, in business, and some extra resources for digging even deeper.

CHAPTER 10

WRAPPING IT UP

It may take some time but having and sticking to a practical and wise plan such as **the 10-10-80 plan** is the path to becoming financially free, whatever your situation. **Give 10%, save 10%, and then live on the remaining 80% or less of your income.**

In every area of life, we usually over-estimate what we can accomplish in one year but we also significantly under-estimate what we can accomplish in a few years or more. It's the same with our finances. Think long term. See the big picture. Get on the right track as soon as possible and then keep going.

Notice that the plan is not the 80-10-10 plan. The order is important. Put God first in your finances then pay yourself. Over time, hopefully you will be able to change the ratios. Why not work towards 15-15-70 and then 20-20-60? It is more possible than you think. If you are in dire straits financially and you are not giving or saving anything at all, you might even start with a 5-5-90 plan simply to create some movement in the right direction.

The 10-10-80 plan is pretty simple, when you think about it. A 10 year old could do it. Then, why isn't everyone doing it? Every person's financial situation is unique. What is right for you may not be relevant for someone else but these principles can work for just about everyone - singles, married couples with no children, married couples with children, single parents, people who are single again (widows and divorcees), and retirees.

My wife, Nicole, and I have used and benefited from these principles for over 30 years of married life. I can tell you, they really work. Recently, we down-sized our family home and now are mortgage-free for the first time in our married life. I can't tell you how much joy and peace that brings.

We have taught these principles to all three of our children. As a result they have become generous people, with significant savings who have all learned to live within their means. As adults in their mid to late twenties now, they are already reaping the reward of managing their finances wisely ever since their early teenage years when we gave them their first pocket money.

The previous church I led used these principles for over 20 years. We gave away a minimum of 10% of our income to ministries outside the church every year. In fact, at one time we were investing up to 37% of our income in local community work and overseas mission. We also ensured we saved a minimum of 10% each year. To achieve this, we established a conservative annual budget for each year that ensured we made a profit by spending less than we earned and then saving the difference. We kept our expenses to 80% or less each year. No wonder the church was so healthy financially - out of debt with money in the bank and at the same time giving generously to local community work, overseas mission activity and completing a number of multi-million dollar building projects debt free. These principles work.

Every healthy business that I know uses these principles too. These financial habits are especially vital for start-up businesses in those first few years but are just as relevant for large multi-national companies.

I could share stories of many people from our church family who have applied these principles and seen incredible breakthroughs in their finances. I am thinking of one man a few years ago who had $13,000 in debt but who within a few years was debt free and with money in the bank because of implementing the 10-10-80 plan in this life. He also saved his marriage in the process.

So what about you?

Your Response?

Where are you in the area of your finances right now?

If you are **doing well financially**, well done! Enjoy the benefits and be a blessing and help to others around you.

If you are **not doing that well**, why not begin making some changes right away. Work back through this book and apply the advice given.

If you are **under financial pressure** or if you have a large amount of debt, talk to a financial advisor and ask for some help to work your way out of your current situation. Don't delay. Make it a priority.

Things More Important than Money

There are many things in life more important than money. In fact, you can have an enjoyable and fulfilling life without having a lot of money. There is a whole lot more to life than money and possessions. Here are three things that are much more important than money:

1. Pleasing God by Living with Integrity

Living with integrity means that there is an integration between the ethical values we espouse to and the way we actually live our life. When there is a gap between the two, we feel a degree of internal stress and unrest. However, when there is no or little gap, we have a greater sense of peace and well-being as we are being true to ourselves and our beliefs.

A life lived well is more valuable and important than wealth or riches. Who you are as a person is much more important than the model of car you drive, the neighborhood you live in, and the amount of money you have in the bank. Keep a proper perspective on money and possessions. We came naked into the world and we take nothing out with us. Let's make sure we live our life in light of eternity and not allow ourselves to live for only temporal things. Here is some more wisdom from the book of Proverbs that teaches us this important truth:

Proverbs 11:4. Riches won't help on the day of judgment, but right living can save you from death. NLT

Proverbs 16:8. Better to have little, with godliness, than to be rich and dishonest. NLT

Proverbs 28:6. Better to be poor and honest than to be dishonest and rich. NLT

2. Enjoying Quality Relationships

People are more important than possessions or things. The lyrics of an old song by American singer B. J. Thomas talk about "using things and loving people, not the other way around." You don't need money to love people and even if you have a lot of money, if you don't have healthy relationships, without love, it means nothing at all. It has no lasting value.

1 Corinthians 13:13. And now these three remain: faith, hope and love. But the greatest of these is love.

Don't let money rob you of investing in your family or friends.

3. Experiencing Inner Peace and Contentment

Contentment is a wonderful thing. It comes from within rather than from a certain set of external circumstances. Of course, contentment is not complacency. You change the things you can and do the things you can do. The things you cannot change you accept and you are content with because you know who is in control. Here are some more wise sayings related to this truth:

Proverbs 15:16. Better to have little, with fear for the Lord, than to have great treasure and inner turmoil. NLT

Proverbs 23:4-5. Don't wear yourself out trying to get rich. Be wise enough to know when to quit. In the blink of an eye wealth disappears, for it will sprout wings and fly away like an eagle. NLT

Ecclesiastes 4:6. Better one handful with tranquillity [peace, rest or quietness] than two handfuls with toil [worry] and chasing after the wind.

Philippians 4:11-13. I am not saying this because I am in need, for I have learned to be content whatever the circumstances. I know what it is to be in need, and I know what it is to have plenty. I have learned the secret of being content in any and every situation, whether well fed or hungry, whether living in plenty or in want. I can do everything through him who gives me strength.

1 Timothy 6:6-10. But godliness with contentment is great gain. For we brought nothing into the world, and we can take nothing out of it. But if we have food and clothing, we will be content [satisfied] with that. People who want to get rich fall into temptation and a trap and into many foolish and harmful desires that plunge men into ruin and destruction. For the love of money is a root of all kinds of evil. Some people, eager for money, have wandered from the faith and pierced themselves with many griefs.

Your Next Step

What you hear or read does not help you unless you do something about it. It is only what we apply and put into practice that leads to lasting change.

C. S. Lewis once said, "We need to be reminded more than we need to be instructed." John Maxwell says, "Most

Christians are educated beyond the level of their obedience." The truth is we already know a lot of things but knowledge does not change the world, action does. Hopefully, these money talks have been a help to you. Ultimately, it is what you *do* with what you now know and have learnt that matters the most.

If we are not careful, we can easily succumb to the materialistic spirit of our age, become prisoners to our debt and be unable to experience the joy of generous giving. Through wise choices we can curb the spirit of greed that so pervades our society (always wanting more), live within our means (spend less than we earn, which is *the* key to financial freedom) and have a generous spirit of giving.

Your journey to becoming financially free begins the moment you make a decision to commit to a commonsense plan. Determine to be a wise steward of your resources - work hard, give generously, save and invest wisely, and spend strategically. I guarantee that you will be glad you did.

May your find increasing amounts of courage, peace and joy as you continue your journey toward financial freedom!

PRAYERS OF FINANCIAL BLESSING

Here are some prayers I have crafted for people in different financial situations.

For those Facing Financial Challenges

"Dear God, I pray for those facing major financial challenges right now. Direct them to some wise counsel. Help them have the courage to do everything they can to get out of destructive debt, even if it means downsizing in order to experience greater peace of mind. As they put you first, bless them financially and bring them to a place of financial freedom, even if it takes a little longer than they would like. Grant them faith and persistence."

For those who are Unemployed

"Dear God, thank you that you give each person the ability and the power to create wealth. I pray for those looking for work that you would give them favor in interviews. Open doors of opportunity and provide just the right job for them that perfectly matches their talents, passions and experience, as well as providing needed income for them."

For Business Owners

"Dear God, I pray for every business owner reading this book - those who are either self-employed or running their own business either as a sole trader or in partnership with others. Running your own business is a tough job. The marketplace is very competitive and unfortunately not everyone goes about their business in an honest way. Finding good staff is not easy either. Work is never done and there is an extra burden that they carry. Assure them that you understand and that you are interested in them as a person and in their business life. Please give them all the faith, wisdom, creativity, innovation, courage and favor that they need for their business. Bless them financially so they can follow the dreams in their heart."

For Employees

"Dear God, thank you for all those who have somewhere to work and add value by providing a service or product. As they work diligently with an excellent attitude and continue to develop themselves, bless them, promote them, give them unexpected bonuses, and meet all of their financial needs. May they find great joy and fulfillment in their vocation."

For those with the Gift of Giving

"Dear God, we are all called to be generous givers but you have given some people a gift of giving. They have a unique ability to make money and a strong desire to bless others and invest in your work. They are energized by giving and find great joy in contributing to vulnerable people and worthy causes. Bless them financially and give them discernment to know where best to invest their resources."

For Everyone

"Dear God, bless each person reading this book. As they honour you in their financial world, open the windows of heaven and pour out a blessing beyond their expectations. May they have the courage to apply the wisdom they have learned so that they may truly be financially free … not only for their own benefit but also for the benefit of others."

APPENDIX 1

REFLECTION AND DISCUSSION QUESTIONS

Following is a list of questions that can be used for personal reflection or for small group discussion.

1. The Bible talks a lot about money. How do you feel about talking about this topic?
2. Reflect on both the dangers and the benefits of wealth.
3. Read Jesus' teaching in Luke 14:28-30 about considering the cost of discipleship and consider what relevance it has to wise financial management.
4. Read Paul's comments on work in 2 Thessalonians 3:6-12 and think about its application to us today.
5. In what situations is it appropriate not to be working and to be dependent on someone else for your income?
6. What are some principles of promotion in the work place? How do Paul's comments in Colossians 3:23-25 relate to this?
7. If you were (or are) an employer, what qualities would you look for when hiring an employee?
8. What are the effects of a Christian employee who under-performs in the workplace?
9. The Bible tells us that Daniel was ten times better than all the other advisors to the king in Babylon (Daniel 1:17-21; 6:3). What are some steps to developing excellence in our work?
10. How can we avoid work becoming an 'idol' (the source of our identity, security and significance)?

11. What are the consequences of neglecting the Sabbath principle and what specific practices can help us to embrace the Sabbath principle?
12. How much work is too much? What are some practical steps we can take to ensure that work doesn't lead to us 'cheating' God or our family?
13. You are offered a higher profile job with significantly more money in another city. What other important factors should you consider *before* deciding whether to take the offer or not?
14. Discuss the quality of contentment and how it relates to work (read Philippians 4:10-13 and 1Timothy 6:6-10).
15. Discuss the problem of gambling. What are some of its causes and consequences?
16. What are the benefits of managing your resources wisely? What are the consequences of not doing so?
17. How can church congregations (including small groups) provide places where each person is encouraged and helped to be blessed financially?
18. Why do you think some Christians struggle with the concept of giving?
19. Share some testimonies that illustrate how giving can release God's blessing in your life.
20. What are some things you would like to do in the future that will require money?
21. Why is saving so hard for most people?
22. What are some lessons about financial investment that you have learned (including both successes and failures) that may be helpful to others?
23. What are some questions we can ask ourselves before buying a particular item (good shopping tips)?

24. What are some ways we can reduce our expenses so we are living within our means?
25. Read Appendix 2 on God's Heart for the Poor and Vulnerable. What can we do to address the issue of poverty today?
26. After reading Appendix 3 about Church Finances, what steps do you think could be taken to improve the financial health of your own local church?
27. Read Appendix 4 on Fundraising Tips and then consider what good causes you could consider giving towards.
28. After reading Appendix 5 about The Purpose of Business, did anything change in your perspective?
29. Look through the Recommended Resources in Appendix 6. Which book or resource could be most helpful to you right now?
30. Finish by praying for financial blessing on your life as you honour God with your finances.

APPENDIX 2

GOD'S HEART FOR THE POOR AND VULNERABLE

"The rich must live more simply that the poor may simply live." Dr. Charles Birch

The Prophet Isaiah

Isaiah, son of Amoz, lived over 2,700 years ago. He was a poetic prophet who spoke of judgment and yet of hope. In Isaiah 58, the question is raised as to whether service to God consists primarily of worship or of works of love for vulnerable people. This question has relevance to every Christian and every church in the world today. Like ancient Israel, we can easily become immune to the desperate needs in our world today. At times, we too need to be stirred from our lethargy and indifference and to seek to meet the needs of people around us – many of them facing things such as poverty, homelessness, and oppression.

Isaiah lived during a time when God's people were very focused on their worship to God – carefully following the right religious rituals. Yet from God's perspective that had forsaken his commands and were in a state of rebellion (see vs.1-3). The evidence of this was the fact that their engagement in religious activities was for their own benefit. Like the pagans, they were seeking to manipulate God to act in their favor. They were getting caught up in things that God had not commanded (like fasts) and were neglecting what God had commanded (compassion for the poor and vulnerable).

The people were fasting at this time to get God's attention and to receive a special blessing from God. Because the benefit had not come, they were complaining to God (vs.3). The prophet considered the people's worship hypocritical because it had no noticeable effect on their daily lives. They were engaging in their worship services and their spiritual disciplines primarily for their own benefit, not for God's.

Isaiah goes on to inform the people that their acts of worship were not enough to please God (vs.4-5). The kind of fasting God desired was not the kind that the people were performing at that time, but a fast that consisted in feeding the hungry, housing the homeless, and clothing the naked (vs.10-11). The purpose of this kind of service was to relieve suffering. That was a service acceptable to God.

Understanding Poverty

According to the World Bank (www.worldbank.org), there has been marked progress on reducing poverty over the past decades. The world attained the first Millennium Development Goal target – to cut the 1990 poverty rate in half by 2015 – five years ahead of schedule, in 2010. According to the most recent estimates, in 2013, 10.7 percent of the world's population lived on less than US $1.90 a day, that's down from 35 percent in 1990.

Around 100 million people moved out of extreme poverty from 2012 to 2013, and since 1990, nearly 1.1 billion people have escaped extreme poverty. The global poor are predominantly rural, young, poorly educated, are mostly employed in the agricultural sector, and live in larger households with more children.

Despite progress, extreme poverty remains unacceptably high, especially in Sub-Saharan Africa. The region now has the largest number of extreme poor in the world, 389 million, which accounts for half of the total number of extreme poor in the world, and more than all the other regions combined. The decline in extreme poverty was largely fueled by the rapid advances in two regions – East Asia and the Pacific and South Asia – specifically in China, Indonesia, and India.

Hunger and starvation still stalk our world. Famine and disease are alive and well on planet earth. There are also new challenges such as AIDS, terrorism, materialism and consumerism, and the breakdown of the family.

God's Heart for the Poor and Vulnerable

It is an interesting exercise to look through the Bible for every single reference to: poor people, to wealth and poverty, to injustice and oppression, and to what the response to all of those subjects is to be from the people of God. Here is what you will discover: There are several 1,000s of verses in the Bible on the poor and God's response to injustice. In fact, it is the second most prominent theme in the Old Testament. The first is idolatry, and the two are often related. 1 in every 16 verses in the New Testament is about the poor or the subject of money. In the first three gospels (the Synoptics), it is 1 out of every 10 verses, and in the book of Luke, it is 1 out of every 7.

If you took a pair of scissors and cut out each one of these verses you would end up with a "Bible full of holes" when it comes to the question of the poor. In the Bible, you will find the poor everywhere, yet the subject has not been very often found in the church. Have we in many ways cut out these verses ... simply by ignoring them or paying no attention to them? Is it possible to really love the Bible, believe that we are basing our lives upon it, and yet be completely missing one of its most central themes?

"Poor" in the Scripture means low economic status usually due to calamity or some form of oppression. Of course, some people are poor because they are lazy and slothful. Revealing the poor is a prophetic task. The poor are there: in God's heart and in Christ's compassion. They are also all around us – if we open our eyes.

The theme of God's heart for the poor and vulnerable continues into the New Testament as well. Just consider Jesus' teaching on who will inherit a place in the kingdom of God (Matthew 25:31-46). It is reserved for those who feed the hungry, welcome strangers, clothe the naked, and visit the prisoners. For Jesus, caring for the poor and outcast is the same as caring for him. In effect, Jesus is saying, "I'll know how much you love me by how you treat them. Whatever you do for them, its like you've done it for me. And conversely, ignoring them is like ignoring me."

Does "the least of these" (vs.45) only refer to Christians who are 'poor believers'? Even if it does, there are other parts of Jesus' teaching that extend the meaning to both believers and unbelievers who are poor and oppressed. The story of the Good Samaritan teaches that anybody in need is our neighbor (Luke 10:29-37).

Paul later says, "Therefore as we have opportunity, let us do good to all people, especially those who belong to the family of believers" (Galatians 6:10). Poverty is not a "left-wing" political issue; it is a Christian issue.

Take a moment to pause and reflect on these proverbs:

Proverbs 14:21. It is a sin to belittle one's neighbor; blessed are those who help the poor. NLT

Proverbs 19:17. If you help the poor, you are lending to the Lord–and he will repay you! NLT

Proverbs 21:13. Those who shut their ears to the cries of the poor will be ignored in their own time of need. NLT

Proverbs 28:27. Whoever gives to the poor will lack nothing, but those who close their eyes to poverty will be cursed. NLT

Proverbs 29:7. The godly care about the rights of the poor; the wicked don't care at all. NLT

Proverbs 31:20. She extends a helping hand to the poor and opens her arms to the needy. NLT

How Should We Then Live?

Sometimes we are tempted to despair or cynicism, thinking that things are hopeless and that nothing we do makes any difference. We can't do everything but we can do something.

Firstly, become more aware of the issues. Inform yourself. Read some good books on these topics (e.g. *Rich Christians in an Age of Hunger* by Ronald Sider, *Make Poverty Personal* by Ash Barker, and *The End of Poverty* by Jeffrey Sachs). See Appendix 6.

Secondly, reflect on your own values and lifestyle. Reject advertising that seeks to seduce you into buying one luxury after another. Distinguish between necessities and luxuries. Don't buy things just because you can afford them. Question your own lifestyle, not your neighbours. Consider simplifying your own lifestyle. Spend less and give more away.

Thirdly, get involved. Take action. There are many reputable organisations committed to the relief of poverty and to helping the oppressed and the vulnerable. Don't just give financially, get involved personally. Make time to serve Jesus through a poor and vulnerable person.

Conclusion

God is not just looking for our worship or our engagement in religious activities. He is looking for our love for him demonstrated through our love for the poor and vulnerable in our world. Ask God to fill you afresh with his compassion. Make justice, love, and mercy your priorities. Be part of the solution.

Discussion and Reflection Questions

1. The Bible refers to God's heart for the poor and the vulnerable frequently. Do you think that this theme is talked about enough in the church or has it been somewhat overlooked?
2. The people in the time of Isaiah were caught up in their worship of God and religious observances. It is possible for us to do the same today? How is this demonstrated?
3. Read and reflect on Jesus' parable of the sheep and the goats (Matthew 25:31-46). Why do you think Jesus made care for the poor and vulnerable *the* issue by which he evaluates his followers in this story – rather than doctrine, personal holiness, or something else?
4. What practical things could you do to demonstrate a greater concern for the poor and vulnerable in our world on a regular basis?
5. Read and discuss these Bible verses: Psalm 41:1-3; 140:12. Proverbs 14:31; 19:17; 21:13. Amos 5:24. James 2:15. 1 John 3:17-18.

APPENDIX 3

CHURCH FINANCES

The church of Jesus Christ has been commissioned to take the good news to all nations. This important task requires resources – people, time, and finances. These resources are primarily provided by the voluntary, generous giving of the members of each local church, who seek to be wise managers of their time, talents, and finances. What follows is a brief overview of what the Bible has to say about finances and then some principles for the church today. We will then talk specifically about how individual churches can manage their finances as an organisation.

Old Testament Times

In Old Testament times, God's people saw him as the owner of everything and themselves as managers of his resources, including their time, talents and finances (1 Chronicles 29:11. Psalm 24:1-2; 50:10-12; 89:11). God was seen as the one who blesses his people with material wealth. However, they were not to trust in their riches in place of him (Psalm 52:2-7). Righteous people were generous givers (Psalm 37:25-26).

Before Moses

From the time of Adam right through to Moses we see a variety of spontaneous voluntary offerings given to God, including by Cain and Abel (Genesis 4:3-7), Noah (Genesis 8:20-22), and Abraham (Genesis 12:7; 13:18). With each of these offerings, there is no percentage mentioned, no amount required, and no frequency referred to. The gifts were prompted by the individual's own initiative, giving out of love and thankfulness to God.

Abraham gave a 'tithe' or tenth of the spoils of a battle he won to a priest named Melchizedek, who he saw as a representative of God (Genesis 14:17-20. Hebrews 7:1-14). This is the first reference to tithing in the Bible. Note that Abraham did not give a tithe of all of his income nor of everything that he owned but only of what he had taken in this particular battle. We also have no record of Abraham doing this in response to a command from God nor do we have a record of him ever doing this again in the 175 years of his life, though he might have. This was a voluntary choice that Abraham made for this occasion motivated by gratitude and generosity.

Jacob also made a vow to give God a tithe of everything he owned but this was at a low point of Jacob's faith and his pledge was more of a bargain or a bribe to try to buy God's blessing (see Genesis 28:20-22). Again, his vow was not in response to a direct command from God or a required percentage. It was a voluntary choice. Also, it may have been for a specific time period, as Jacob only refers to his journey and then his anticipated return to his father's house in this vow.

The only required giving during this period was the collection of 20% (a fifth) of all produce for a period of seven years. This was directed by God to support the nation of Egypt under Joseph's leadership as a solution to an upcoming period of severe famine (Genesis 41:25-36). It was essentially a national tax to help supply the future needs of the people.

After Moses

From Moses onwards we have the time of the Law and tithing becomes a familiar term during this period, whereas it was only mentioned two times prior to this (Abraham and Jacob). After the time of Moses, we see two types of giving: **required giving** and **voluntary giving**.

Required giving included the tithe, which was a 10% taxation system on all produce. They lived in an agricultural society so they gave of their crops, herds, and flocks. This was used to supply the needs of the Levites who oversaw the Temple activity and ran the theocratic nation of Israel (Numbers 18:25-32. Leviticus 27:30-33). The Levites were the priests who had no other income and who received no land as an inheritance. This was referred to as the Levite tithe.

There was also a second annual tithe that the Israelites had to pay which was to support the national religious festivals, such as Passover. It was to be taken to Jerusalem and was to be eaten by family and friends. It was to stimulate devotion to God and it promoted national unity and fellowship (Deuteronomy 12:1-32; 14:22-27). This was referred to as the festival tithe.

There is also reference to a third tithe that occurred every three years (Deuteronomy 14:28-29). This was known as the welfare tithe, or poor tithe, and was used to help the foreigner, the fatherless, and the widowed. There was also a profit-sharing tax (see Leviticus 19:9-10) that involved leaving some of the fruit from their fields for the poor and vulnerable (that is what Ruth was doing in the fields in the Book of Ruth).

Finally, there was the requirement for Sabbath rest of the farm land every seventh year (Exodus 23:10-11) where the normal earnings for an entire year were forfeited so that the soil could rejuvenate itself.

So the average Israelite was required to provide a Levite's tithe, a festival tithe (to support the national religious program), a welfare tithe (for the poor), a profit-sharing tax, a Sabbath for the land every seventh year, and an annual Temple tax (which was a third of a shekel).

All of this adds up to more than 25 percent in annual income tax to the national theocratic government of Israel.

It was far more than the simple 10 percent that has often been cited as an argument for required tithing today. It is interesting to note that the government of most nations today tax their people in approximately the same range (20-30%).

All of this was required giving. These were not voluntary offerings. Tithing was not really 'giving' because the tithe belonged to God anyway. If the Israelites did not give their tithe, they were robbing God (see Malachi 3:8-12). Tithes were not primarily gifts to God, but taxes that contributed to the national budget in Israel.

In addition to the required giving mentioned above, there were times when the Israelites gave **voluntary freewill offerings**. With voluntary giving, the emphasis was not on the quantity or the percentage of the gift but on the attitude of the giver and the quality of his or her gift. They were proportionate (according to the individual's personal resources and whatever they chose to give), generous, and sacrificial offerings from willing hearts. This included the first-fruits offering (Numbers 18:1-32. Deuteronomy 26:1-15. Nehemiah 10:35-39. Proverbs 3:9-10) and offerings for the construction of the tabernacle (Exodus 35:4-9, 20-29; 36:1-7) and later on the temple under David's leadership (1 Chronicles 29:9). This freewill giving often exceeded the need at hand (see Exodus 36:1-7). The people gave willingly and there was great joy in it.

New Testament Times

The New Testament picks up on these themes. Jesus told his disciples that they were managers or stewards of God's resources and that they would be held accountable for their faithful use (Luke 12:42-48; 16:1-13). This included a disciple's time, talents, and finances. Jesus made it clear that his followers were to surrender all to follow him (see Luke 14:3; 18:22) and that everything needs to be constantly available for his use. Jesus also taught frequently about money and possessions, warning of the potential dangers of wealth (Luke 16:1-5) while encouraging his followers to be generous givers (Matthew 6:1-4; 19-24. Mark 12:41-44. Acts 20:35).

The book of Acts tells the story of the birth and expansion of the early church. Generous giving was an evidence of God's Spirit at work amongst believers (Acts 2:41-47; 4:36-37; 11:27-30). The church community entrusted its financial giving to its leadership for proper care and distribution (Acts 4:34-35; 11:30). Finances were used to help the vulnerable (Acts 2:42-47; 4:32-5:10) and to assist other church communities (Acts 11:27-30. 1 Corinthians 16:1-4). Later on the apostle Paul encouraged the giving of financial support for church leaders and teachers (1 Corinthians 9:11-12. 1 Timothy 5:17-18), although he did not demand this for himself.

Paul spent considerable time raising funds for various needs, including those affected by a famine in Jerusalem (Galatians 2:10). The church in Corinth had expressed their desire to be a part of this (1 Corinthians 16:1-2) but had not followed through with their giving. Paul wrote to the church to urge them to complete their commitment to generous giving (2 Corinthians 8-9).

Generous giving was always a part of the life of a follower of Jesus. From the narratives and instructions about giving in the New Testament, we can derive the following principles of financial giving for Christians today. Note that some of these are repeated in Appendix 4 about fundraising due to them being drawn from the apostle Paul's comments in relation to his fundraising efforts for the poor at Jerusalem.

Principles of Financial Giving

Where to Give

In the first century, Christians gave to help the poor and vulnerable (Matthew 25:25. Acts 11:28-30. Galatians 2:9-10. 1 Corinthians 16:1-3. 2 Corinthians 8-9 and also Romans 15:25-27), to support preachers of the gospel and the leaders of the church (Matthew 8:22; 10:10. 1 Corinthians 9:7-14. Gal.6:6. 1 Timothy 5:17-18. 2 John 5-8), and to meet each other's needs (Acts 2:42-46; 4:32-35).

In each local church, it is beneficial if each person gives first of all to the general church account which helps to provide resources for the core activities of the church - teaching, pastoral care, outreach, as well as various administrative expenses. In addition to this, individuals may choose to donate additional designated offerings to other activities such as local community outreach, international mission work, and poverty relief.

Church members may also choose to give to other ministries outside of their own local church but it really helps when their first priority is toward their own home church. As with a natural family, it is important to support your own spiritual family where you are cared for, taught and given opportunities to serve.

How Much to Give:

Jesus made it clear that his followers were to surrender all to follow him (see Luke 14:3; 18:22). Christian giving is based on the understanding that all that we have belongs to God (100%). We are to see ourselves as managers of someone else's resources.

Give proportionately. For a follower of Christ, giving amounts are personally determined. There is no amount stipulated. Zacchaeus, a rich tax collector, chose to give

50% of his goods to the poor and paid those he had stolen from four times as much (Luke 19:8). Neither Jesus nor Paul ever set a certain percentage as a minimum or a maximum amount for giving. Giving was to be a spontaneous expression of love and gratitude, "according to their means" and "in keeping with their income (1 Corinthians 16:2. 2 Corinthians 8:11-12)." If someone has little, then they are to give of what they have. If a person has much, then they are to give of what they have. People gave according to their ability as they decided in their heart (Acts 11:28-30).

Giving from a willing heart according to one's resources may mean 10% for some and even more than 10% for others, but it does not condemn others who may not be able to give that much. I recommend 10% as a practical amount for the majority of people, based on *principle* rather than command. Most churches ask their members or partners to commit to giving at least 10%, as an expression of their discipleship and support for their local church. If each church member simply gave 10% of their income on a regular basis, each local church would have more than enough resources for the mission they have been given.

Give generously. Believers were to use wisdom and to give in relation to their income, but they were also encouraged to give generously, even sacrificially (2 Corinthians 8:20; 9:5-6). A sacrifice is something that costs us something (2 Corinthians 8:2-5). Jesus set the supreme example (2 Corinthians 8:9). The widow gave a very small amount, but Jesus noted that she gave her all and more than the rich who gave out of their abundance (Mark 12:41). A small amount may be given in a sacrificial way and this is what moves God's heart (Hebrews 13:16. Philippians 4:18). I encourage people to give generously to their home church so that the work of God will be well-resourced. I truly believe that those who give in this way will receive God's blessing on their own lives as a result.

How to Give:

First all, give willingly. Giving is to be voluntary and from the heart. No one is to give to God or his work because they feel they have to. There is never to be a sense of pressure or obligation. When Paul was raising funds he was looking for willingness, an eagerness to help, and enthusiasm, not reluctance or a sense of obligation, coercion or compulsion (2 Corinthians 8:3-5, 8-9, 12; 9:1-2, 6-8). The same is seen in all occurrences of giving recorded in the book of Acts. God's Spirit moved people's hearts to give unselfishly, generously, and without pressure. Giving is to be an act of love. It is so encouraging when people give willingly to the work of the church, out of love for God, love for people, and a desire to see the church fulfill its mission.

Secondly, give regularly. When Paul was raising money he wanted people to be ready and prepared to give. They were to set aside a sum of money during the week and bring it to the church gathering where it would be collected (1 Corinthians 16:1-2). The decision was not made under pressure but before the church meeting. He wanted them to make a wise, calculated decision that had a faith and sacrificial component to it. He wanted them to avoid quick, hasty decisions. He wanted them to pray and consider their own financial situation then come ready to give (2 Corinthians 9:3).

Although spontaneous giving is to be encouraged, planned giving is also important. I believe that regular, consistent giving is good stewardship of what God has given us. I encourage church members to honour God with the first portion of any income that they receive. This helps to avoid giving becoming something haphazard or in response to emotion alone.

Thirdly, give cheerfully. God loves a cheerful giver (2 Corinthians 8:2-3; 9:6-8. Romans 15:25-27). This refers to a giver who is excited about giving, knowing that as they invest in God's kingdom, they are going to make a difference in the lives of other people.

It is encouraging when church members see giving as an opportunity to be a part of God's great work in the earth. This is not to be drudgery or a chore. It is a joy to invest our lives in something that really matters - helping to build the church of Jesus Christ, which has been entrusted with the Gospel which is the only thing that can change a human heart.

Fourthly, give wisely. Believers were to ensure that the church leaders took good care in handling the money given and that there was appropriate accountability (2 Corinthians 8:18-21). Auditors and guardians were appointed for proper financial accountability and responsibility.

Integrity should be a high value in every local church, especially in the area of finance. Systems and processes of accountability need to be in place for the appropriate collecting, spending, and reporting of all financial matters. Also, any time people are encouraged to give, it should be done without any sense of manipulation or pressure.

Fifthly, excel in giving. Followers of Christ are to be good at giving - not only the other aspects of the Christian life, such as faith, speech, knowledge, earnestness and love (2 Corinthians 8:7).

Desire to be a generous giving person in every area of your life - time, service and finance. Giving provides for people's needs, is an expression of thanks to God, and causes people to praise God (2 Corinthians 9:12-14).

These are the clear principles of Christian giving as outlined in the New Testament. The apostle Paul wrote:

2 Corinthians 9:7-8. You must each decide in your heart how much to give. And don't give reluctantly or in response to pressure for God loves a person who gives cheerfully. And God will generously provide all you need. Then you will always have everything you need and plenty left over to share with others." NLT

To Tithe or Not to Tithe?

Tithing refers to the giving of 10% of one's income to the work of the church. The word 'tithe' is derived from an old English word that means '10 percent' of one's income. Both the Hebrew and Greek equivalents are mathematical words meaning 'a tenth'.

There has been a lot of debate about tithing over the years. There are **three main views:**

1. Some churches and preachers believe that all of the Old Testament laws of tithing still apply to Christians today. They believe that if Christians don't tithe they are under a curse and will not receive the blessing of God in their lives (see Malachi 3:8-12). I even heard of one preacher who said that there were people who were sick in his church – because they had not been tithing faithfully.

2. Other churches and preachers believe that the Old Testament teaching about tithing is no longer relevant for Christians today and that we are no longer under these laws. There are plenty of books and articles out there against tithing.

3. Personally, I believe that Jesus came to set us free from the curse of the law. We are not under the Old Covenant any more. Of course, under the New Covenant, everything (100%!) that we have is to be

seen as belonging to God and available for his use at any time. I believe that 'tithing' - giving 10% of our income to the work of God - is an excellent *principle* of good financial management (not a *law*).

As we already noted, Abraham, the "father of all who believe" (Romans 4:11), gave a tithe of the spoils of a battle he won (Genesis 14:20), well before there was any law about tithing (under Moses). The teaching in the New Testament about giving focuses on generosity. We give, not because we *have to* (out of a sense of duty) or because we are afraid of being judged if we don't, but because we *want to* - voluntarily and willingly (see Paul's teaching in 2 Corinthians 8-9). **Giving 10% of our income to God's work is the starting point to a life of generosity.**

Every local church benefits from church members who commit to support the work of God through the church by giving 10% of their income. Without this financial giving, churches could not do the ministry they are involved in today. In fact, if *every* church member simply gave 10% of their income to their local church, the church would have more than enough money for the vision and the ministries they have.

Notice that even Jesus commended the Pharisees for handling their giving well (Matthew 23:23). They went the extra mile. They did not think about how little they could give. Jesus affirmed them for this, while challenging them to not neglect the more important matters of the law, such as justice, mercy and faithfulness.

Management of Church Finances

Accountability

Good stewardship is a corporate responsibility not just an individual responsibility. Each local church is responsible to manage the resources that God has given them through the voluntary donations of their members. The church does not exist to make money; rather, to take all that it receives and to invest it wisely into areas of ministry that will have a high return for the kingdom of God.

Accountability is an important aspect of the management of church finances. Ideally, each year something similar to an Annual General Meeting is held and, amongst other things, an audited annual financial report is presented to the members (partners) of the church. At this meeting, it is beneficial for partners to be given a copy of the audited accounts of the church for the past financial year and have the opportunity to ask any questions they may have.

Usually, a team of Elders or a Board of Directors provide the spiritual oversight of each local church and are responsible to hold the Senior Pastor accountable for overseeing all aspects of the various ministries of the church, including the day-to-day financial management of the church and the management of expenditure of various areas according to previously agreed upon budget allocations throughout the year.

How to Give

Usually donations can be made to a local church via giving envelopes, cash or checks given during the weekly offering time, via credit card or via online giving or the church app. Designated offerings can often be made to specific ministries such as local community work, overseas mission work, poverty relief or building programs.

Financial Stewardship

I believe that pastors and churches should teach their people, not just about giving, but also about the broader principles of financial management, similar to what we have covered in this book. This can be done through teaching series, special seminars, and membership classes, as well as regular offering talks.

Conclusion

Church governance and the management of church finances are vital parts of any healthy church community. The leadership of each local church needs to be committed to handling these matters with wisdom and integrity. As they do so, each local church will be well-positioned and well-resourced to pursue its God-given mission.

APPENDIX 4
FUNDRAISING TIPS

Many people and groups engage in fundraising today, including businesses, not-for-profit organizations and churches. In this section I want to share some lessons I have learned about raising money. By God's grace, along with the help of others on the leadership team and the generosity of many people, I have seen millions of dollars raised for local community work, overseas mission, and a number of building programs (one costing 7 million dollars that I was able to see completed debt free and another project costing 11 million dollars which I helped to launch and raise the initial funds for).

Personally, I am very aware of how sensitive this topic of money and giving is. It is not something we should do lightly or without prayer and thought. I am very aware that there is a lot of cynicism in the world today about the church and some people believe that the church is always asking for money. I also understand that people don't have the same resources and some are struggling financially. However, I also have this sense of faith and confidence inside of me that motivates me to rise above any sense of fear and boldly encourage people to step out in faith and obedience in this area of giving. It's not about equal giving - it's about equal sacrifice, each of us doing what God tells us to do - nothing more and nothing less. We want people to sacrifice luxury not basic living, to be radical but not reckless.

Don't look at fundraising merely through natural eyes. See with the eyes of faith. We are not the source - God is. We are simply his channel. He can flow money *to us* if he can flow money *through us* into his work. We have nothing to lose and everything to gain by putting our trust completely in God and his ability to supply finances for the worthy causes he puts on our heart. Our faith is not in money. A lot of people have faith *in* finance. I believe God wants us to have faith *for* finance – believing him for what we do not yet see and what may seem impossible to the natural mind.

My Top Ten Tips for Raising Funds

1. **Have a compelling cause.** People need an inspiring vision to give towards. They need to know *why* they should give and what outcome their generosity will achieve. Without a sense of urgency about the need, it will be difficult to motivate people to give. Engage all the key influencers in creating and agreeing to this cause. The greater the level of ownership you can create, the more solid your base of support will be before you even start.

   Of course, it is vital that you personally believe in the project you are presenting to other people. You need to know deep inside that it is worthwhile and that it will really make a difference in the lives of people. In fact, you need to believe in it enough to invest your own personal resources into it, leading by example in your own generous giving.

   A project name or tagline can be helpful. The first building project I led was called "Building Our Future" and it was all about making more space for each ministry of the church, including expanding the auditorium, the foyer, the children's rooms and the cafe. A later project we called "The Story Building Project." Buildings don't change peoples lives but what happens in them can and does. We were making room for more stories of transformation to take place. A missions fundraiser we conducted had the stated purpose of planting 100 new churches in some off the most unreached areas overseas. Be creative in how you present your fundraising project and make sure it comes across as inspiring as possible.

2. **Choose your financial target wisely.** Choose a stretch goal without it being an unattainable goal that will only discourage people. Most churches can raise an amount equal to one to two times their annual income over a one to two year period. I think it is better to under-project and then over-perform than to set the bar too high only for everyone to feel like they failed in their fundraising efforts.

3. **Break the financial target down into achievable steps.** Create bite size chunks so that each person can see how they can make a helpful contribution. For instance, a million dollars can seem like an insurmountable amount of money and even beyond reach in the average person's mind. However, if 500 people gave $19.24 a week for two years (which equates to $1,000.48 each per year or $2,000.96 each over two years), then you would raise over a million dollars. Some may not be able to give this much while others could give much more. This sort of breakdown makes it doable. It is amazing what a group of people can do together when they rally around a common goal.

4. **Teach people *how* to give.** Give them creative ideas for where the funds could come from. For instance, people can give of what they already have set aside in savings. Or they can earn more money and give from the profits. I know of a single mother who rented out a bedroom and a teenager who mowed lawns to raise money to give towards a worthwhile cause.

People could sell some of their assets. In the early church in Jerusalem, a man named Barnabas sold a piece of land he owned and gave the proceeds to the leaders to distribute where most needed (Acts 4:32-37. See also Acts 2:45). Fundraising provides an opportunity for each person to put everything they own 'on the table' as it were, making it available for God's use. People can have a garage sale or put some unwanted items up for sale on eBay. I know a pastor who sold his boat and gave the proceeds to his church's building fund. Another idea is to go without something, thereby reducing expenses, and then give some or all of those funds.

5. **Share stories along the way.** Stories inspire people. Celebrate the wins. We don't give in order to get but often when people do give, God blesses their lives. Share these stories as encouragement for people to keep giving in faith.

6. **Keep reinforcing the vision.** Don't over-vision people but do make sure they hear the *why* behind what you are doing frequently enough to keep the momentum going. After the initial launch of the project, it is easy to get caught up in the details of the project. Keep lifting people's eyes to the long-term results that will be achieved when the project is completed.

7. **Keep people informed with the progress made.** Accurate and up-to-date information is important. Inform people of the progress made in the fundraising journey.

8. **Make adjustments along the way**. We make our plans but rarely does everything go exactly to plan. Observe the process closely, listen carefully to people's thoughts and feelings, and make any needed adjustments, whether that be to the process itself, the strategy you are using or even the end target.

9. **Right-size your expectations**. It is good to have faith but faith needs to be partnered with wisdom. Aim for the best you can but work with what you have. Don't place your expectations so high that you set yourself up for disappointment, which other people will feel.

10. **Celebrate what is achieved and give thanks to everyone involved**. Small wins and achievements matter. Every dollar counts and makes a difference. Be grateful for every person who gives and every amount of money that comes in. That's good news, whatever way you look at it.

Biblical Principles of Fundraising

As noted already earlier in this book, I believe that the Bible is God's Word to us and because it is inspired by the Holy Spirit it is beneficial for every aspect of life. We know that the Bible has a lot to say about our personal finances but what about fundraising? Interestingly enough, the apostle Paul spent many years raising funds for a need in the city of Jerusalem. In this appendix, we will look at how he went about this and draw some lessons for today. [This will be applied primarily to churches endeavoring to raise money but there is broader applicability to all other organizations]

The apostle Paul was an amazing person. He had a personal encounter with Jesus Christ that changed his life forever. He became a preacher of the gospel, a missionary, a church planter, an apostolic leader overseeing numbers of churches, a theologian who received revelation about God's purpose and plan for the world, a spiritual father to many and a trainer of others.

Paul was also a fundraiser who spent a fair amount of time raising money for various projects, especially for some needs within the church at Jerusalem. This is referred to in his letters as "the collection". Paul gave some detailed instructions to these churches concerning their giving (see (1 Corinthians 16:1-3. 2 Corinthians 8-9. Romans 15:25-27). These instructions were given specifically to churches in the area of Galatia and the city of Corinth.

Like all things in the Bible, these things are written for our benefit and our instruction. Some of these principles were mentioned in Appendix 3 on Church Finances but they are worth repeating here in the context of fundraising.

1. Give Willingly

Giving to any good cause is to be done voluntarily and willingly. No one has to give. It is entirely up to each individual person to choose whether they want to be involved or not.

> *2 Corinthians 8:8-9. I am not commanding you, but I want to test the sincerity of your love by comparing it with the earnestness of others.*

> *2 Corinthians 8:3-5. Entirely on their own, they urgently pleaded with us for the privilege of sharing in this service to the saints.*

Here we have God moving on people's hearts so that they voluntarily and willingly choose to give to the cause Paul was raising funds for. He was looking for people who were eager to help, those with enthusiastic hearts. He did not want anyone to feel pressured or obligated to give.

> *2 Corinthians 8:12. For if the willingness is there, the gift is acceptable according to what one has, not according to what one does not have.*

> *2 Corinthians 9:1-2. There is no need for me to write to you about this service to the saints. For I know your eagerness to help, and I have been boasting about it to*

the Macedonians, telling them that since last year you in Achaia were ready to give; and your enthusiasm has stirred most of them to action.

2 Corinthians 9:6-8. Each person should give what they have decided in their heart to give, not reluctantly or under compulsion, for God loves a cheerful giver.

It was the same with building projects recorded in the Old Testament. God gave a vision to his appointed leaders. They shared it with the people. The people's hearts responded and they gave willingly.

Exodus 25:1-2. The LORD said to Moses, "Tell the Israelites to bring me an offering. You are to receive the offering for me from each man whose heart prompts him to give.

Exodus 35:5. From what you have, take an offering for the LORD. Everyone who is willing is to bring to the LORD an offering of gold, silver and bronze.

Exodus 35:20-23. Then the whole Israelite community withdrew from Moses' presence, and everyone who was willing and whose heart moved him came and brought an offering to the LORD for the work on the Tent of Meeting, for all its service, and for the sacred garments. All who were willing, men and women alike, came and brought gold jewellery of all kinds: brooches, earrings, rings and ornaments.

The people brought so much day after day that the building foremen had to tell Moses to get them to stop. He had to restrain the people from giving.

Exodus 36:6-7. Then Moses gave an order and they sent this word throughout the camp: "No man or woman is to make anything else as an offering for the sanctuary." And so the people were restrained from bringing more, because what they already had was more than enough to do all the work.

What an incredible story of the generosity of people giving towards a cause that they believed in. A similar thing happened during the time of King David as people gave out of their devotion to God's house.

1 Chronicles 29:1-9. Then King David said to the whole assembly, "... with all my resources I have provided for the temple of my God ... then the leaders ... gave willingly ... the people rejoiced at the willing response of their leaders, for they had given freely and wholeheartedly to the Lord."

I had a similar experience with the Building Our Future project at my last church. We ended up raising all of the $7 million dollars needed for the project. The building was completed (on time and on budget) and we had money in the bank yet some people still had outstanding pledges they had not yet met. I will never forget the weekend I stood up in church and informed the people that we as the leadership team had decided to release them from their remaining pledges. We had 'more than enough' for the project. They could stop giving now. The people cheered. Yes, and news spread far and wide and some pastors called me and said I was crazy! No, I was simply thankful for the way God blessed a project that was well led and for a church of willing, generous givers.

2. Everyone Should Consider Giving

Although Paul did not want to pressure anyone to give to his fundraising efforts, he did expect everyone who was a part of the church communities he was in relationship with to at least consider giving something. Notice the use of the words "each one".

1 Corinthians 16:2. On the first day of every week, each one of you should set aside a sum of money in keeping with his income, saving it up, so that when I come no collections will have to be made.

2 Corinthians 9:7. Each person should give what he or she has decided in their heart to give, not reluctantly or under compulsion, for God loves a cheerful giver.

Paul encouraged willing and voluntary giving but he wanted each person to consider giving. It is like you don't have to give but you really should! He believed strongly in the cause he was raising money for and therefore he believed that everyone should contribute. He desired unity of vision and purpose amongst his churches.

Hopefully, the cause you are raising money for is something that everyone involved within your church or group will consider contributing towards. If you are part of a church family, then you really should strongly consider being involved. Can you in good conscience stand on the sidelines and let others do all the work and then you simply enjoy the benefits without contribution?

You might have heard the story about four people named Everybody, Somebody, Anybody and Nobody. There was an important job to be done and Everybody was sure that Somebody would do it. Anybody could have done it, but Nobody did it. Now Somebody got angry about that because it was Everybody's job. Everybody thought Anybody could do it, but Nobody realised that Everybody wouldn't do it. It ended up that Everybody blamed Somebody when Nobody did what Anybody could have done. When there is no commitment, Nobody does it!

In any church or organisation, if only a few people contribute that will not be enough to achieve most financial goals. God is a miracle working God and any target is achievable but it usually takes *everybody* to consider making a contribution. It is easy for people to think that somebody else is going to do it. They need to know that you need them to help out.

It is always sad and unfortunate when people who could give withhold their donations for instance to church building projects for various reasons and then continue to enjoy the benefits of everyone else's giving. I believe when everyone benefits, everyone should contribute. I could not in good conscience be part of a church that was building and not contribute (if I had the resources to do so) and then simply enjoy the benefits of everyone's sacrifice. Unfortunately, some people do exactly this.

3. Prepare to Give

Notice Paul's instructions here:

> *1 Corinthians 16:2. On the first day of every week, each one of you should set aside a sum of money in keeping with his income, saving it up, so that when I come no collections will have to be made.*
>
> *2 Corinthians 9:3. But I am sending the brothers in order that our boasting about you in this matter should not prove hollow, but that you may be ready, as I said you would be. For if any Macedonians come with me and find you unprepared, we-not to say anything about you- would be ashamed of having been so confident. So I thought it necessary to urge the brothers to visit you in advance and finish the arrangements for the generous gift you had promised. Then it will be ready as a generous gift, not as one grudgingly given.*

Paul expected people to be ready and prepared to give. They were to set aside a sum of money during the week and bring it to the church gathering where it would be collected. The decision was not to be made under pressure but before the church meeting where the offerings were received. They were to bring their donation(s) with them. Gifts were not collected at home.

Any time I have led fundraising projects, I have established a multi-week period of prayer because I think it is important that each person have time to think about and prepare for their decision as to what to give. One week is too short and a few months starts to drag out. A good prayer to encourage people to pray during this time is, "Lord, what do you want to do through me to accomplish your work through this project?"

We want people to make a wise, calculated decision that has a faith and sacrificial component to it. Being wise and intelligent means avoiding quick, hasty decisions that one may regret later. Asking people to pray, consider their own financial situation and come ready to give or pledge helps people to do this.

4. Give Proportionately

Paul wanted people to give "according to their means". People can only give out of what they have, not what they don't have. It is healthy when people mix *faith* with *wisdom* when they choose what amount they will give. Paul's desire was equal sacrifice not equal gifts.

> *1 Corinthians 16:2. On the first day of every week, each one of you should set aside a sum of money in keeping with his income, saving it up, so that when I come no collections will have to be made.*
>
> *2 Corinthians 8:3. For I testify that they gave as much as they were able.*
>
> *2 Corinthians 8:11-13. Now finish the work, so that your eager willingness to do it may be matched by your completion of it, according to your means. For if the willingness is there, the gift is acceptable according to*

what one has, not according to what one does not have. Our desire is not that others might be relieved while you are hard pressed, but that there might be equality.

Paul wanted equality, not one person being hard pressed while others were relieved. Each person's contribution makes a difference. It is amazing how much you can raise when everyone gets involved and does their part.

If a person has little, then encourage them to give of what they have. Small gifts matter to God. Think of the story of the widow giving a small coin into the Temple treasury yet Jesus commended her for her generosity to God's work (Mark 12:41-44). Make sure each person knows that no gift is too small. Of course, if people have been blessed with much, they should be encouraged to give accordingly.

5. Give Generously

Paul encouraged people to be generous in their giving.

2 Corinthians 8:20. We want to avoid any criticism of the way we administer this liberal gift.

2 Corinthians 9:5-6. So I thought it necessary to urge the brothers to visit you in advance and finish the arrangements for the generous gift you had promised. Remember this: Whoever sows sparingly will also reap sparingly, and whoever sows generously will also reap generously.

Generosity often involves sacrifice, giving something or an amount that costs us something. That is what people in the churches in Galatia did during Paul's fundraising project.

2 Corinthians 8:2-5. Out of the most severe trial, their overflowing joy and their extreme poverty welled up in rich generosity. For I testify that they gave as much as they were able, and even beyond their ability. And they did not do as we expected, but they gave themselves first to the Lord and then to us in keeping with God's will.

Jesus set the supreme example by becoming 'poor' so that others might be 'rich' (2 Corinthians 8:9). Out of our riches we can give so others may be blessed even if it means that we have less for ourselves.

The amount is not always as significant as is the level of sacrifice. The widow gave a very small amount, but Jesus noted that she gave her all, and more than the rich who merely gave out of their abundance (Mark 12:41-44). King David said that he would not give to God that which "cost him nothing" (2 Samuel 24:24).

Many years ago, Dr. Cho from Korea launched an inspiring vision for a new church building. When they began to build, the Middle East war broke out. The economy of the country was affected and businesses were running at a loss. As a result of lack of funds the church could not pay the builders and the work had to be stopped. The structure of the building slowly began to decay. The pastor was heartbroken.

The church fasted and prayed earnestly seeking God's direction. One very cold winter day they gathered together to pray. An elderly lady from church about 80 years old started trembling, came up and asked to speak to the group. Pastor Cho noticed that she had something in her hand wrapped in a piece of newspaper. Pastor Cho was hesitating to give her the microphone but she was persistent. She claimed she had something to offer. Reluctantly Pastor Cho gave her 5 minutes to speak. As she picked up the microphone she started crying and said that she was a widow and she didn't have any children and that she was living on welfare. She was grateful for the ministry of Pastor Cho as she came to know Jesus through his ministry. She began to unwrap the parcel in her hand and it was an old rice bowl and chop sticks. It was something she inherited that was passed down through the generations. That was her only valuable possession and she decided to offer it to God that he might build his church.

Pastor Cho was touched by her offering and asked what she was going to use to eat from now on and her reply was that she had a cardboard box that she can use instead. Dr Cho refused the offer saying that he simply could not accept it, as it was the only valuable possession of this poor window. She was offended by the Pastor's response thinking that he did not value her offering. The pastor in his heart felt very saddened by this and suddenly to his amazement, a businessman stood up and offered $3,000 to purchase the rice bowl then one by one people began to offer $5,000, 10,000, 30,000, 100,000 and so on. Pastor Cho praised God for what he was doing through this widow and his dream came alive again. The spirit of brokenness came upon the people and they pledged homes, lands and in some cases one year's salary and everything they had. That day alone they raised $2 million. Pastor Cho expected the miracle to come from a distant place but it was right there in their midst. The people gladly gave as they were moved by he power of the Holy Spirit and they raised enough to finish the building in spite of the circumstances.

That's an inspiring story of sacrificial giving that overflowed into generosity. When people's hearts are moved to give like this, incredible things can be accomplished. Even when we give what seems like a little, doing our best, God can do amazing things.

6. Give Joyfully

Paul wanted people to give joyfully. Here is an opportunity to go down in history, to be a part of God's great work in the earth. History makers are risk takers who boldly step out in obedience to God's promptings.

This is not to be drudgery or a chore. It is a joy to invest our lives in something that really matters – helping to build the church of Jesus Christ.

> *2 Corinthians 8:2-3. Out of the most severe trial, their overflowing joy and their extreme poverty welled up in rich generosity. For I testify that they gave as much as they were able, and even beyond their ability.*
>
> *2 Corinthians 9:6-8. Each person should give what they have decided in their heart to give, not reluctantly or under compulsion, for God loves a cheerful giver. NLT*
>
> *Romans 15:25-27. Now, however, I am on my way to Jerusalem in the service of the saints there. For Macedonia and Achaia were pleased to make a contribution for the poor among the saints in Jerusalem. They were pleased to do it, and indeed they owe it to them. For if the Gentiles have shared in the Jews' spiritual blessings, they owe it to the Jews to share with them their material blessings.*

Giving to a good and worthy cause is going to make a difference in someone's life. You are investing for a better world. What a joy that should be.

7. Ensure Financial Accountability

Paul wanted to ensure that the church leaders involved in his fundraising project took good care in how they handled the money that was given.

> *2 Corinthians 8:18-21. We are also sending another brother with Titus. All the churches praise him as a preacher of the Good News. He was appointed by the churches to accompany us as we take the offering to Jerusalem—a service that glorifies the Lord and shows*

> *our eagerness to help. We are traveling together to guard against any criticism for the way we are handling this generous gift. We are careful to be honorable before the Lord, but we also want everyone else to see that we are honorable. NLT*

Paul used reputable people with an excellent reputation for their character to collect the money. Integrity was vital. Auditors and guardians were appointed for proper financial accountability and responsibility.

Integrity should be a high value in every church and organization, as well as every fundraising endeavor. This includes establishing proper systems and processes of accountability for all money collection (at least two people should count all monies given), as well as how the money is spent (it is good practice to require two signatures for all checks written, a completed requisition form for all expenditures, and a budget to be accountable to). In addition, there is often a need for regular financial reports and audited accounts. How we go about raising funds is very important too. Don't make any use of hype, manipulation or pressure.

8. Excel in the Grace of Giving

Paul wanted the people in his churches to be good at giving, not just the other aspects of the Christian life.

> *2 Corinthians 8:7. But just as you excel in everything-in faith, in speech, in knowledge, in complete earnestness and in your love for us-see that you also excel in this grace of giving.*

God is a great giver. He gave generously, willingly and sacrificially. He is the first giver. He gave his Son unselfishly for our benefit. All Christian giving is our response of gratitude for God's generosity to us.

2 Corinthians 8:9. For you know the grace of our Lord Jesus Christ, that though he was rich, yet for your sakes he became poor, so that you through his poverty might become rich.

2 Corinthians 9:15. Thanks be to God for his indescribable gift!

We are to be like God. This means becoming generous giving people in every area of our life - our time, our service and our finance. Giving provides for people's needs, is an expression of thanks to God and causes people to praise God.

2 Corinthians 9:12-14. So two good things will result from this ministry of giving—the needs of the believers in Jerusalem will be met, and they will joyfully express their thanks to God.

As a result of your ministry, they will give glory to God. For your generosity to them and to all believers will prove that you are obedient to the Good News of Christ. And they will pray for you with deep affection because of the overflowing grace God has given to you. NLT

Provision for the Vision

I believe that God wants to give provision for the vision he has for each ministry, organisation and local church. God's resources are unlimited. He is not limited by our resources. He will supply all our needs according to his riches (Philippians 4:19). He can turn a few loaves and fishes into enough to feed thousands of people, water into wine at a wedding feast, and a small jar of oil and flour into food for a single mother's family and for Elijah.

We do the possible (give of what we have) and he does the impossible (multiplies it to meet the need at hand).

This is how God works. He resources us out of our acts of faith, not our millions of dollars.

If each person simply does their part and obeys what God tells them to give, then it is amazing how much money you can raise. I truly believe there will be more than enough.

Giving is not just about sacrifice. It positions us to receive some tremendous blessing. God blesses and helps those who invest in and help to build his purpose on planet earth. God is the God of re-supply

57 Cents - A True Story

Here is one final story to encourage you in your fundraising efforts.

A sobbing little girl stood near a small church from which she had been turned away because it 'was too crowded'. "I can't go to Sunday School", she sobbed to the pastor as he walked by. Seeing her shabby, unkempt appearance, the pastor guessed the reason and, taking her by the hand, took her inside and found a place for her in the Sunday School class. The child was so touched that she went to bed that night thinking of the children who have no place to worship Jesus.

Some two years later, this child lay dead in one of the poor tenement buildings and the parents called for the kind-hearted pastor, who had befriended their daughter, to handle the final arrangements. As her poor little body was being moved, a worn and crumpled purse was found which seemed to have been rummaged from some trash dump. Inside was found 57 cents and a note scribbled in childish handwriting which read, "This is to help build the little church bigger so more children can go to Sunday school." For two years she had saved for this offering of love. When the pastor tearfully read that note, he knew instantly what he would do.

Carrying this note and the cracked, red pocketbook to the pulpit, he told the story of her unselfish love and devotion. He challenged his deacons to get busy and raise enough money for the larger building.

But the story does not end there. A newspaper learned of the story and published it. It was read by a realtor who offered them a parcel of land worth many thousands. When told that the church could not pay so much, he offered it for 57 cents.

Church members made large subscriptions. Checks came from far and wide. Within five years the little girl's gift had increased to $250,000.00 - a huge sum for that time (near the turn of the century). Her unselfish love had paid large dividends.

When you are in the city of Philadelphia, look up Temple Baptist Church, with a seating capacity of 3,300, and Temple University, where hundreds of students are trained. Have a look, too, at the Good Samaritan Hospital and at a Sunday School building which houses hundreds of Sunday scholars, so that no child in the area will ever need to be left outside during Sunday school time. In one of the rooms of this building may be seen the picture of the sweet face of the little girl whose 57 cents, so sacrificially saved, made such remarkable history. Alongside of it is a portrait of her kind pastor, Dr. Russel H. Conwell, author of the book, "Acres of Diamonds" - a true story.

Goes to show what God can do with just 57 cents!

Conclusion

This story shows a huge impact through the life of one little girl who was willing to give what she had to benefit others. This is much like the little boy who offered his lunch to Jesus so a multitude would be fed.

Believe in the vision and the cause you are seeking to raise money for. Have faith for it. Be confident about it. Encourage people to seize the moment. Pray for participation and ownership of everyone giving in wisdom with faith and sacrifice.

Pray for those who have already decided what they will give that God will provide for them and bless them according to their generosity.

Pray for those who are still considering what they will give that God would speak very clearly to them and they would obey what he tells them to give.

Pray for those who are not planning on contributing that the Holy Spirit would touch their heart and prompt them to be involved.

Pray for those few people who may be cynical, critical or negative about your fundraising project that God would touch and soften their hearts to see the value in the project and that they would be a positive partner in it.

Pray that people who are on the fringe will move from going to church to being a part of your church and from consumers to contributors.

I am believing with you for great things!

APPENDIX 5

THE PURPOSE OF BUSINESS

I enjoy spending time with and speaking to business owners and managers. I know that as leaders in business they carry a far greater weight of responsibility than the average employee. For most, this challenge is an exciting and enjoyable experience but it also creates an added burden at times that can be quite draining and even stressful.

Thankfully, God is very interested not only in our personal lives but in our work and our business. Following is the basic content of a message I shared at a business leaders' breakfast a few years back.

Business - Secular or Sacred?

Unfortunately, many people have created a division between what is seen as 'sacred' and what is 'secular'. In fact, there has been a certain amount of tension between business and Christianity throughout the centuries. Let's quote a few famous early church leaders:

> St. Jerome said, *"A merchant can seldom if ever please God."*
>
> St. Augustine, a fifth century bishop, wrote, *"Business is in itself evil."*

That's not that encouraging if you are involved in business! This dualistic worldview is a product of Greek philosophy that has so influenced our Western worldview. Life is often seen as a series of *boxes* - one for family, one for work, one for friends, one for recreation, and one for religion (God or our 'spiritual life'). As long as we prioritize correctly and make appropriate contributions to each box, life will work out for us. This results in compartmental thinking. Our faith and our relationship with God are seen as 'sacred'. Everything else is viewed as 'secular' (having no religious, sacred or spiritual aspect).

In contrast, in the Hebrew mind, and therefore in biblical thinking, life should be viewed as one large circle with God in the centre. Everything else is to find its meaning and perspective from that centre. God wants to be involved in every area of our life - not just our spiritual life. All of life is sacred and God is interested in every dimension of our lives. All of life is to be lived in his presence and for his pleasure.

Brother Lawrence is well known for writing a little booklet that has touched millions of people's lives. It's called *Practicing the Presence of God*. It's about living with a greater realization each moment of every day that God is with us and interested in doing life (including work) together with us.

The apostle Paul put it this way:

> *Colossians 3:17. And whatever you do or say, let it be as a representative of the Lord Jesus, all the while giving thanks through him to God the Father. NLT*

Doing something in Jesus' name means to do it in his character. It means doing it as Jesus himself would do it if he were in your place. Paul is saying that our entire lives - from the moment we wake up until the time we lay down to sleep - are to be lived out 'in the name of Jesus'. That is what genuine discipleship is all about. In all of our life we are to honour and represent Jesus Christ. This includes our business.

Your business is sacred. It is part of God's purpose for your life.

> *Genesis 1:26-30. Then God said, "Let us make man in our image, in our likeness, and let them rule over the fish of the sea and the birds of the air, over the livestock,*

over all the earth, and over all the creatures that move along the ground." So God created man in his own image, in the image of God he created him; male and female he created them. God blessed them and said to them, "Be fruitful and increase in number; fill the earth and subdue it. Rule over the fish of the sea and the birds of the air and over every living creature that moves on the ground." Then God said, "I give you every seed-bearing plant on the face of the whole earth and every tree that has fruit with seed in it. They will be yours for food. And to all the beasts of the earth and all the birds of the air and all the creatures that move on the ground – everything that has the breath of life in it – I give every green plant for food." And it was so.

God's mandate for us in creation was to take dominion over the earth and to work productively in it.

Genesis 2:15. The LORD God took the man and put him in the Garden of Eden to work it and take care of it.

Work was God's intention for us before and after sin entered the world. It was not a curse given to us because of sin. Business is simply the institutionalisation of work.

Many of the people God used in the Bible had careers and ran businesses at some stage in their life. They were not all 'people of the cloth' or working in the Temple or the church environment.

- Abraham was a herder of vast flocks of sheep, goats, donkeys, cattle, and perhaps even camels. Many modern scholars think he was also a trader, managing donkey caravans and doing business from Turkey to Egypt.
- Deborah was a judge in Israel.
- David was a king, responsible for an entire nation.
- Nehemiah was an employee in the king's palace.

- Daniel was a government official.
- Amos was a farmer.
- Jesus was a carpenter up until the age of 30. He had to deal with customers, products, suppliers and orders.
- Paul was a tentmaker who funded his church work through the profits he made (in partnership with Aquila and Priscilla).
- Peter, James and John were fishermen who had a fishing business with their father.

God is interested in our relationships in the workplace and how people treat each other. The apostle Paul wrote about the relationship between masters and slaves back in the time of the Roman Empire but this instructions also contain timeless and relevant principles for the workplace today.

> *Ephesians 6:5-9. Slaves, obey your earthly masters with deep respect and fear. Serve them sincerely as you would serve Christ. Try to please them all the time, not just when they are watching you. As slaves of Christ, do the will of God with all your heart. Work with enthusiasm, as though you were working for the Lord rather than for people. Remember that the Lord will reward each one of us for the good we do, whether we are slaves or free.*
>
> *Masters, treat your slaves in the same way. Don't threaten them; remember, you both have the same Master in heaven, and he has no favorites. NLT*

What is the Purpose of Business?

So what is God's purpose for business? Let's look at **four major aspects of why your business exists** as a Christian:

1. To Glorify God

Who we are and how we do business should please God and bring glory to him.

> *Matthew 5:13-16. "You are the salt of the earth. But what good is salt if it has lost its flavour? Can you make it useful again? It will be thrown out and trampled underfoot as worthless. You are the light of the world – like a city on a mountain, glowing in the night for all to see. Don't hide your light under a basket! Instead, put it on a stand and let it shine for all. In the same way, let your good deeds shine out for all to see, so that everyone will praise your heavenly Father. NLT*

We are God's representatives in the world and we need to represent him in such as way that we bring him praise and honour.

> *Deuteronomy 4:5-8. "You must obey these laws and regulations when you arrive in the land you are about to enter and occupy. The LORD my God gave them to me and commanded me to pass them on to you. If you obey them carefully, you will display your wisdom and intelligence to the surrounding nations. When they hear about these laws, they will exclaim, 'What other nation is as wise and prudent as this!' For what great nation has a god as near to them as the LORD our God is near to us whenever we call on him? And what great nation has laws and regulations as fair as this body of laws that I am giving you today? NLT*

The way we live and do business should attract people to God and give us opportunities to point people to him. It is possible to be ethical and successful (though it takes more than ethics to guarantee success).

> *Micah 6:8. The Lord has told you what is good, and this is what he requires of you: to do what is right, to love mercy, and to walk humbly with your God. NLT*

Here are **three ways to bring glory to God**:
a. **Act justly** - do what is right, fair and equitable.
b. **Love mercy** - be kind in the way you treat people.
c. **Walk humbly** - don't become arrogant or prideful (something that wealth and success can tend to produce).

Everything about us is part of God's message through us to the world. How we treat others - our customers, our competitors and our community - speaks volumes to people.

> *Colossians 4:5-6. Be wise in the way you act toward outsiders; make the most of every opportunity. Let your conversation be always full of grace, seasoned with salt, so that you may know how to answer everyone.*

2. To Serve People

Every business, and therefore every job, should exist to add value - to provide a service or a product that enhances people's quality of life.

> *Matthew 20:28. The Son of Man did not come to be served, but to serve, and to give his life as a ransom for many.*

> *Galatians 5:13. For you have been called to live in freedom, my brothers and sisters. But don't use your freedom to satisfy your sinful nature. Instead, use your freedom to serve one another in love. NLT*

Your business or the industry you work in does not exist only as a way to make a living but as part of God's plan for meeting the needs of people and making the world a better place. Your organization exists for its customers not just its owners or shareholders. Great service creates not just customers, but raving fans who are so excited about the way they were treated that they brag about the organization and its service.

Think about Jesus who attracted crowds of people without all of our modern day marketing methods (advertising, flyers, etc). Why? He knew and met real needs and people kept spreading the word until he had more customers than he could handle. Talk about customer service! God wants us to do the same thing.

When we make a delicious meal, clean a house, construct a building, create something of artistic beauty, make a more reliable vacuum cleaner or a more fuel efficient car, we are doing kingdom business.

3. To Provide an Opportunity for Meaningful Contribution

God has created us with the need for meaningful work. Part of our sense of significance comes from our ability to make a contribution to our world. God is a worker and he created us to work too. It is part of his purpose for our lives. Your business can provide people with an opportunity to be involved in meaningful work, thus enhancing their sense of dignity and contribution.

> *2 Thessalonians 3:6-13. And now, dear brothers and sisters, we give you this command with the authority of our Lord Jesus Christ: Stay away from any Christian who lives in idleness and doesn't follow the tradition of hard work we gave you. For you know that you ought to follow our example. We were never lazy when we were with you. We never accepted food from anyone without paying for it. We worked hard day and night so that we would not be a burden to any of you. It wasn't that we didn't have the right to ask you to feed us, but we*

> *wanted to give you an example to follow. Even while we were with you, we gave you this rule: "Whoever does not work should not eat." Yet we hear that some of you are living idle lives, refusing to work and wasting time meddling in other people's business. In the name of the Lord Jesus Christ, we appeal to such people – no, we command them: Settle down and get to work. Earn your own living. And I say to the rest of you, dear brothers and sisters, never get tired of doing good. NLT*

By creating and maintaining jobs we provide work that not only supports families financially but also harnesses people's skills and creative energies.

4. To Generate Wealth

By this time, some of you are asking, "Where's the money?" Well, here it is. In exchange for service or a product, we receive payment of some sort. This is the principle of fair exchange. It's okay to make a profit. Making a profit simply enables you to do business for another day.

> *Deuteronomy 8:18. But remember the LORD your God, for it is he who gives you the ability to produce wealth, and so confirms his covenant, which he swore to your forefathers, as it is today.*

With the profit we make we can reward ourselves and our staff, as well as have resources to invest back into the business and to contribute towards God's work in the earth.

Learning to Lead Like Jesus

As business leaders, we want to learn and grow so that we can become the very best we can be. There is a plethora of business gurus and materials available to help us (Bill Gates, Jack Welch, Peter Drucker, and Patrick Lencioni, for example). Simply walk into your local bookshop and look in the business/management section. There are dozens of experts sharing their latest ideas (TQM, 360 degrees, Balanced Scorecard, etc) on how to see your business break through to new heights of productivity and success. Even most Christian leaders today glean much from the corporate and business world for wisdom in building their churches and organizations.

We can also learn from other Christians in business, especially from those who are more experienced than ourselves. However, our ultimate business model and leadership example is Jesus Christ.

Isn't it funny that we often look to everyone but the greatest leader who has ever lived - Jesus Christ! Sure he didn't have an office, a mobile phone, a web site or a business card, but his enterprise, the church of Jesus Christ, has had unparalleled growth and longevity. From humble beginnings, it has continued to expand for over 2,000 years. That's what I call built to last! It has a strong international presence and yet is as local as the neighbourhood street corner. Its capital resources are beyond measure and its membership beyond counting. And what a membership! Many have given their lives to show their loyalty. Yes, Jesus was a carpenter. Yes, he was a preacher. But his life and his work also just happen to offer some of the most insightful business advice a manager could ever find.

We are all looking for relevant and competent role models for effective leadership. Jesus is the greatest management-entrepreneur ever. He is the perfect practitioner and teacher of effective leadership. He had the right heart, the right methods and the right behaviour. He was more than a good man and a great teacher. He is the most relevant leadership model and teacher for our daily lives that there is.

I can hear you thinking, "What does Jesus know about my business?" (computers, marketing, graphics, property, wholesale, retail, accounting, etc). That's just what a man named Simon Peter thought. In Luke 5, we have the story of Jesus giving him some advice for his fishing business. Jesus said, "Put out into deep water and let down your nets for a catch." Imagine what Peter was thinking right then. "Look Jesus, you seem to be a great teacher, but now you're talking about my area of expertise. Fishing is my business. What you're asking us to do isn't practical. Besides, it's going to be a lot of hard work and we'll probably have to pay overtime." Anyway, Peter says, "Master, we've worked hard all night and haven't caught anything. But, because you say so, I will let down the nets."

Peter quickly learned that Jesus knew a lot about fishing too. What a catch - a net breaking, boat sinking, record setting catch! Jesus knows your business too and he can help you. **Jesus is the best leadership model that there is.** Think about the things he modeled:

1. MBWA (management by walking around) - Jesus sure did this a lot. He wasn't stuck in an office all day.
2. Eating with the troops. Jesus did this.
3. Head hunting - Jesus pulled out all the stops to fill a key spot. He personally went to recruit a key player on the opponent's team, Saul. He didn't worry about what his current employees would think either.
4. Preparation is essential. Jesus prepared for 30 years for 3 years of impact.
5. Pay your taxes. Jesus did (Luke 20:25).
6. Remain calm in the storm.
7. Prepare for your successors.

All of us need to learn to lead like Jesus.

Business management expert Ken Blanchard (author of the best selling book *The One Minute Manager*) is a committed Christian who is now focusing his life on helping people to learn to lead like Jesus (see his web site www.leadlikejesus.com).

The world is in desperate need of a different leadership role model. We live in a world where the pursuit of money, recognition and power dominate the leadership landscape. Leadership has become all about self-promotion (pride) and self-protection (fear) in an "It's all about me" world. Many leaders act as if the sheep are only there for the benefit of the shepherd.

The good news is that there is a better way. Jesus is the one leadership model you can trust. He can teach you how to lead in a way that honours God and restores health and effectiveness to organisations and relationships. Jesus calls us to 'servant leadership'. It's not an option for Christ-followers. It's a mandate.

Ken Blanchard describes 'leading like Jesus' as a process of transformation that requires the alignment of four leadership domains: the heart, the head, the hands and the habits.

The first two are internal domains - the motivations of your heart and the leadership perspective of your head - that are things you keep inside of you. The external domains - your public leadership behavior, or hands, and your habits as experienced by others - will determine whether people will follow you. When these four domains are aligned, extraordinary levels of loyalty, trust and productivity will result. Learning to lead like Jesus can be a transformational journey.

Conclusion

In conclusion, God is interested in your business. It is sacred, not secular. There are four purposes of your business - to glorify God, to serve people, to provide opportunity for meaningful contribution and to generate wealth. Finally, learn to lead like Jesus - with your heart, your head, your hands and your habits. Make this your life pursuit.

Discussion and Reflection Questions

1. Reflect on your work and the business you are involved in – what do you enjoy about your job and what is frustrating about it?
2. What does the fact that God is a worker tell us about his nature and character?
3. Although God gives dignity and purpose to our work, we know that sin has affected everything. Think about the challenges and potential frustrations of work in a fallen and broken world (read Genesis 3:16-19 and Ecclesiastes 2:17-20).
4. Consider the common divide between 'sacred' and 'secular' What are some practical ways you can include and be more aware of God in the daily routines of your life?
5. What does it look like to do our daily work "in Jesus' name?"
6. How can our work bring glory to God (read and reflect on Deuteronomy 4:5-8. Matthew 5:13-16. Micah 6:8. 1 Corinthians 10:31 and Colossians 4:5-6 for some ideas)?
7. What are some criteria to consider when contemplating a potential job, career or business selection?
8. How can retirees continue to make a contribution - without retiring from life?

APPENDIX 6

RECOMMENDED RESOURCES

In this final appendix I would like to acknowledge some of the sources of many of my ideas about money, in addition to the biblical texts we have examined in this book. I love learning, so I am an avid reader and listener of others. Over the years I have gleaned a lot of wisdom and insight from many people, including on the topic of money. Below is a list of some of those resources. I am sure you will see the influence that these people have had on my thinking throughout what I have written in this book.

Of course, recommendation is not full endorsement. Learning is a lot like eating fish - eat the meat and spit out the bones. However, ultimately all truth is God's truth and the key is to get wisdom, from wherever it may come.

52 Offering Prayers and Scriptures by Frank Damazio (Portland, Oregon: City Christian Publishing, 1999).

Achieving Financial Freedom - an audio teaching series by Bill Hybels from Willow Creek Community Church in Chicago.

The Barefoot Investor: The Only Money Guide You Will Ever Need by Scott Pape (Melbourne, Australia: John Wiley & Sons, 2017).

Beyond Tithing by Stuart Murray (Tyrone, GA: Paternoster Press, 2000).

Business Through the Eyes of Faith by Richard C. Chewning (San Francisco, CA: HarperOne, 1990).

The Cashflow Quadrant by Robert T. Kiyosaki (Plano, TX: Plata Publishing, 2011).

Contagious Generosity: Creating a Culture of Giving in Your Church by Chris Willard and Jim Sheppard (Grand Rapids, MI: Zondervan, 2012).

Effective Church Finances: Fundraising and Budgeting for Church Leaders by Kennon L. Callahan (New York, NY: John Wiley & Sons, 1992).

The End of Poverty: Economic Possibilities for our Time by Jeffrey Sachs (New York, NY: Penguin Books, 2005).

The Eye of the Needle: Discipleship and Wealth by Jim Reiher (Springvale, Australia: UNOH, 2005).

Following God's Financial Plan: What To Do When the Economy Stinks - an audio teaching series by Rick Warren from Saddleback Church in California, USA (2001).

Giving and Stewardship in an Effective Church by Kennon L. Callahan (New York, NY: John Wiley & Sons, 1997).

God at Work: Live Each Day with Purpose by Ken Costa (Nashville, TN: W. Publishing Group, 2016)

Good Sense: Biblical Principles for Transforming Your Finances and Your Life by Dick Towner (Grand Rapids, MI: Zondervan, 2002).

Jesus CEO: Using Ancient Wisdom for Visionary Leadership by Laurie Beth Jones (New York, NY: Hachette Books, 1996).

Keys to Financial Excellence by Dr. Phil Pringle (Dee Why, Australia, PaX Ministries, 2003).

Lead Like Jesus: Lessons from the Greatest Leadership Role Model of All Time by Ken Blanchard and Phil Hodges (Nashville, TN: Thomas Nelson, 2008).

Make Poverty Personal: Taking the Poor as Seriously as the Bible Does by Ash Barker (Grand Rapids, MI: Baker Books, 2009).

Making Money: The Keys to Financial Success by Paul Clitheroe (Melbourne, Australia: Penguin Books, 2011).

The Management Methods of Jesus: Ancient Wisdom for Modern Business by Bob Briner (Nashville, TN: Thomas Nelson, 1996).

The Millionaire Next Door by Thomas J. Stanley and William D. Danko (New York, NY: Rosetta Books, 2010).

The Money Diet - Reaping the Rewards of Financial Fitness by Ginger Applegarth (New York, NY: Viking Publishing, 1995).

Money Matters in the Church: A Practical Guide for Leaders by Aubrey Malphurs and Steve Stroope (Grand Rapids, MI: Baker Books, 2007).

Neither Poverty Nor Riches: A Biblical Theology of Possessions by Craig L. Blomberg (Downers Grove, IL: InterVarsity Press, 1999).

Personal Financial Management: Gaining Control of Your Finances - an audio teaching series by John C. Maxwell Ministries (El Cajon, CA: INJOY).

Proven Principles of Successful Stewardship - an audio teaching series by John C. Maxwell (El Cajon, CA: INJOY, 1994).

Rich Christians in an Age of Hunger by Ronald J. Sider (Nashville, TN: Word Publishing, 1997).

Rich Dad Poor Dad by Robert Y. Kiyosaki (New York, NY: Warner Books, 1997).

Tithes and Offerings by Kevin J. Conner (Melbourne, Australia. KJC Publications, 1993).

Tithing by R. T. Kendall (Grand Rapids, MI: Baker Books, 1983).

The Total Money Makeover by Dave Ramsey (Nashville, TN: Thomas Nelson, 2003).

The Treasure Principle: Unlocking the Secret of Joyful Giving by Randy Alcorn (New York, NY: Penguin Random House, 2001).

When Work and Family Collide: Keeping Your Job from Cheating Your Family by Andy Stanley (Colorado Springs, CO: Multnomah Books, 2002).

Whose Money Is It Anyway? by John MacArthur (Nashville, TN: Word Publishing, 2000).

Your Money Matters by Malcolm McGregor (Minneapolis, MN: Bethany House Publishers, 1997).

ABOUT MARK CONNER

Mark Conner is a gifted leader, speaker, and author with over three decades of church leadership experience. After serving 32 years on staff at CityLife Church in Melbourne, including 22 years as Senior Minister, Mark now focuses on speaking, writing, coaching, and consulting. He holds qualifications in business, theology, ministry, coaching, and supervision. Mark is passionate about helping people grow and thrive. He is married to Nicole, and they enjoy family life with their three adult children and their grandchildren.

Visit www.markconner.com.au for more information about Mark's ministry, including details of his speaking schedule and links to videos of his messages.

Mark's books are available in paperback format from www.word.com.au and in paperback and eBook format from www.amazon.com/author/markconner

CONTACT:
Email: mark.conner7@icloud.com

HOW TO AVOID BURNOUT
PRINCIPLES OF HEALTHY LIVING

In a world of rapid change, growing complexity and increasing pressure, stress and burnout are becoming far too common. In this practical book, Mark Conner shares five habits for healthy living, gleaned from his decades of experience as an organizational leader and Christian minister.

"This book is both timely and important ... It is well researched and written with very practical guidelines and a rich set of biblical and other references."
Keith Farmer, B.Comm., B.A. (Hons), D.Min.
Former Principal of Australian College of Ministries

PASS THE BATON
SUCCESSFUL LEADERSHIP TRANSITION

There is no success without a successor and Christianity is always one generation away from extinction. These two sobering facts highlight the urgent need for successful leadership transition in today's churches and ministries. CityLife Church (formerly Waverley Christian Fellowship) is a church that has successfully navigated three leadership transitions in its fifty year history. In this informative and practical book, Mark Conner shares vital principles and lessons to help you be more effective with any leadership transition.

[The Amazon editions include a brief Postscript from 2017 regarding Mark Conner's own transition]

PRISON BREAK
FINDING PERSONAL FREEDOM

Living in our broken world creates the possibility of becoming trapped by various negative emotions and habits that can easily become like a prison around us. In this helpful book, Mark Conner shares practical principles for finding freedom from common problems such as anger, fear, worry, rejection, depression, addictions, and spiritual bondages. With God's help you can make a prison break - beginning today.

"The book is practical yet sound, both psychologically and biblically and easy to read. I am sure no reader will be disappointed."

Archibald D. Hart.
Fuller Theological Seminary

TRANSFORMING YOUR CHURCH
SEVEN STRATEGIC SHIFTS

If there was ever a need for a healthy, relevant and dynamic churches to emerge, it's right now In today's culture of constant change, how is it possible for a church to remain relevant and effective? In this book, Mark Conner reveals seven strategic shifts that every church must make in order to be effective in the 21st century. These principles will help your church play a vital role in extending the kingdom of God to impact communities, cities and nations for his glory.

"Mark Conner is a superb leader and communicator whose vision has led to remarkable growth in his own church. I am so grateful for his friendship and inspiring example.

Nicky Gumbel
Holy Trinity Brompton and ALPHA International

SUCCESSFUL CHRISTIAN MINISTRY

The Bible teaches that every Christian is a minister. In fact, the church needs more ministers not just more members. Only as every believer discovers their spiritual gifts and begins to serve passionately will we see the church rise up to fulfill its destiny to take the gospel to the nations of world and be salt and light in each local community. If there ever was a time for every Christian to rise up and take their place in effective ministry, it's right now.

What are the keys to building a high impact long lasting ministry? In this book, Mark Conner shares seven principles for building a successful Christian ministry drawn from his years of ministry experience and observation. Each chapter is packed with practical advice that will empower you to reach your God-given potential and to make a positive difference in the lives of other people.

THE SPIRITUAL JOURNEY
UNDERSTANDING THE STAGES OF FAITH

When you are on a journey, it helps to have a map of the terrain and a guide to help you along the way. In this book, Mark Conner presents such a map and guides us through the stages of faith that are common to the spiritual journey. This journey is rarely linear or in a straight line. There are many curves, twists and surprises along the way. Sometimes we seem to move in circles or in random patterns that don't make sense at the time. Nevertheless, God is at work in our lives. Welcome to the journey of faith.

www.ingramcontent.com/pod-product-compliance
Lightning Source LLC
Chambersburg PA
CBHW020659220526
45464CB00001B/499